THE DEVIL'S CROWN

Henry II and his sons, from a drawing after Matthew Paris. (British Library)

THE DEVIL'S CROWN
A History of Henry II and His Sons

Richard Barber

COMBINED BOOKS
Pennsylvania

For information, address:
COMBINED BOOKS
151 East 10th Avenue
Conshohocken, PA 19428

Library of Congress Cataloging-in-Publication Data
Barber, Richard W.
The devil's crown: a history of Henry II and his sons / Richard Barber.
p. cm.
Originally published: London: British Broadcasting Corp., 1978.
Includes bibliographical references and index.
ISBN 0-938289-78-0
1. Great Britain—History—Angevin period, 1154-1216. 2. Henry II, King of
England, 1133-1189. 3. Richard I, King of England, 1157-1199. 4. John, King
of England, 1167-1216. 5. Great Britain—Kings and rulers—Biography. I. Title.
DA206.B34   1996
941.03'03'1092
[B]—DC20   96-19308

Printed in the United States of America

CONTENTS

Maps/Charts

Chapter 1

A Royal Inheritance

*T*wenty miles south of the river Loire and its châteaux, in the wooded hills of Touraine, stands the abbey of Fontévrault. Here, beneath the echoing grey stone domes of the abbey church, lie the effigies that mark the graves of Henry II, Eleanor of Aquitaine and Richard I, alone between bare walls. How did these three great figures from England's history come to be buried in a remote French abbey?

The story of Henry and his sons, the 'Angevin' kings of England, begins in the confused politics of France in the tenth century. France was ruled by a number of local lords, and the king in Paris had only the most shadowy control over what his barons did on their own lands. Two of the most energetic of these noble families were the dukes of Normandy and the counts of Anjou. The Norman dukes had been Viking seafarers only a century earlier, and had won their lands by conquest, exchanging their swords for ploughs and their longboats for farms, after their leader Rollo had been bought off by King Charles the Simple in 911 with the grant of rich lands along the Channel coast. Rollo or Hrolf, called the Walker by his Viking comrades because he was so huge that no horse could carry him, founded the dynasty of the Norman dukes.

The Normans transformed the face of Europe in the next century, spreading as far as Italy, Sicily and Jerusalem itself; nearer to home, they brought England back into the sphere of Continental politics just when it seemed that it might become part of the Scandinavian world, remote from the mainstream of European events.

Interior of the 12th century abbey at Fontévrault. (Archives Photographiques)

Even after William's conquest of England, the island kingdom might easily have regained its independence, for his sons Robert and William Rufus divided his lands in 1087, and Normandy was only reunited with England after Robert had been defeated at the battle of Tinchebrai in 1106, by William Rufus' son Henry I. Robert dragged out the rest of his life in prison, dying at Cardiff in 1134, and with his death the last threat to the union of Normandy and England seemed to have disappeared.

The Normans made an immense impression on their contemporaries. Just as their Viking ancestors had struck terror into the hearts of half Europe by their raids, so the Normans inspired a mixture of awe and admiration by their energy and political skill. An

Italian contemporary, watching them carve out a kingdom for themselves in Sicily and southern Italy, wrote:

> The Normans are a most cunning race, taking revenge for injuries in the hope of profiting from them, despising those who till the fields, eager for gains and power, deceiving in all things, wavering between generosity and meanness. Their princes enjoy the greatest of good reputations; they are a people who know how to flatter, and who devote themselves to the study of eloquence, so that you listen even to their boys as you might listen to trained speakers. Although they have to be compelled to obey the law, they are untroubled by hard work, hunger or cold, when these are inflicted on them; they are patient as well. They are devoted to hunting and hawking. They delight in splendid horses and other equipment of war, as well as in fine clothing.

The counts of Anjou had a less spectacular background, but they had nonetheless acquired considerable territory over the centuries. Starting as viscounts of Angers, they had gradually extended their lands eastwards until they met the rival ambitions of the counts of Blois. Southwards, they had pushed beyond the Loire to the boundaries of the county of Poitou, while to the north lay the county of Maine, coveted by both them and the Normans; but it was the Angevin counts who won it, by a marriage alliance in the late eleventh century. Fulk V, having achieved this coup, went on crusade and ended his days as king of Jerusalem.

The house of Anjou was now one of the five great families of northern and western France: the French kings, the dukes of Normandy and Aquitaine, the counts of Anjou and Blois. As such they acquired their own family legends. Medieval men thought of society as an unchanging order, where everyone had his place. Any exceptional success could only be ascribed to superhuman interference: the awe in which the great lords were held gave rise to strange stories. The counts of Anjou, noted for fiery temper and ruthlessness, could only come from the devil, and so their line was traced back to a demon ancestress, wife of Geoffrey Greygown, one of the earliest counts.

No one knew where she had come from; Geoffrey had married her solely because of her beauty, for which she was famous. She came only rarely to Mass, and this was much remarked on in an age when regular attendance at church was expected. When she did come, she seemed uneasy, and always left just after the gospel was read, avoiding the central moment of the service, the elevation of the Host. The count determined to see what would happen if she stayed, and ordered four men to hold her back when she tried to leave. As usual, she turned to leave after the gospel, but the men seized her cloak; at which she slipped out of it and flew out of the window with a scream, never to be seen again. Such legends were not uncommon: the lords of Lusignan in Poitou, whose rise to power was similar to that of the counts of Anjou, had a demon ancestress called Mélusine. But they marked the family in question as something out of the ordinary run of mere mortals.

In normal circumstances, the Norman and Angevin rulers would have been deadly rivals, and there was no love lost between their subjects, who had fought spasmodically along the border between Maine and Normandy. However, Count Fulk of Anjou, in his anxiety to depart on crusade, decided in 1119 to marry his daughter to Henry's son William Audelin, giving Maine as the dowry, in the hope of securing his son Geoffrey's position as count of Anjou by a treaty with his formidable neighbor. William was now to be ruler of an even wider empire than his father, with Anjou as an ally rather than an enemy.

But Henry I's plans for his united realm of England and Normandy came suddenly to grief. He had spent four years in Normandy, and in November 1120, he and his court were returning to England. They sailed from Barfleur, on the northern tip of the Cotentin peninsula, in the late afternoon of 25 November. The sea was calm, and the weather fine, with a favorable wind. The king and his companions left first; William Audelin, and the younger members of the court stayed behind for a drinking session that went on until nightfall. They counted on the speed of their vessel, *The White Ship*, to catch up with the king. By the time they embarked, both passengers and crew were drunk, and although the night was clear and moonlit, the helmsman steered the ship onto a rock in the middle of the bay. Within minutes it had begun to sink, and William and a few companions scrambled into the ship's boat and began to row away. They turned back for a moment to pick up one of William's half-sisters, and were at once overwhelmed by other members of the company trying to clamber aboard. The boat sank;

and only one man, who survived by clinging to the ship's mast, lived to tell the story of the disaster.

Henry was a widower, and although he married again after William's death, he had no more children. His only other legitimate child was Matilda, who had been married at the age of eight to the German emperor, Henry V. The emperor died in 1126, and Henry summoned Matilda back to Normandy. She was reluctant to leave Germany, which she had come to regard as her home, and where she was both honored and popular. The humbler circumstances of Henry's court provided a sharp contrast. There, she was merely a pawn in her father's plans to rebuild a continuing Anglo-Norman empire.

Although no woman had ever ruled England or Normandy in her own right, in January 1127 Henry made his barons swear allegiance to Matilda as his successor. There was nothing very unusual in this. Women had often inherited feudal estates in their own right, and even the greatest duchies passed to heiresses without dispute: the French duchy of Aquitaine was to have a duchess on the death of Duke William IX in 1137. Henry had secured his first objective; and later that year he re-established the alliance with Anjou by arranging a marriage, which took place in 1128, between the twenty-five-year-old Matilda and the fourteen-year-old heir to Anjou and Maine, Geoffrey.

Matilda and Geoffrey made an uneasy pair. Geoffrey was well read, like other members of his family, subtle and patient, not caring greatly for the outward trappings of his position. His nickname, Plantagenet, is said to have come from his habit of wearing a spring of broom (*planta genista* in Latin) when out riding. Matilda was never known by such familiar names: to the end of her days she remained the Empress, proud, and overbearing to the point of stupidity, but brave and tenacious as well. There were rumors of a permanent separation within a year or two. Despite this, Matilda bore Geoffrey three sons: the eldest, Henry, was born at Le Mans in March 1133, while his brothers were a year and three years younger.

As his grandfather had planned, the young Henry was heir to a vast empire, almost as large as France itself. But being the eventual heir and actually claiming that inheritance were very different matters. When Henry was two, his grandfather fell ill and died after a week's illness; and at once his carefully laid schemes fell apart. The barons had sworn allegiance to Matilda out of awe for her father, in whose commanding presence only the boldest would have resisted. They were as uneasy about Matilda, with her haughty foreign ways, as she was about her new husband and kingdom.

Among the barons who had taken the oath was Henry's nephew Stephen, brother of the count of Blois. If Matilda was not to inherit, the next claimant was strictly Stephen's elder brother, count Theobald; but Theobald was content with his own wide lands south-west of Paris, and it was Stephen who decided to try his luck and resist Matilda's accession. As soon as news of Henry's death reached him he crossed the Channel and seized the two vital centres of English government, the treasury at Winchester and London itself. With the help of Hugh Bigod, one of the most powerful of the English barons, he persuaded the archbishop of Canterbury to crown him king, even though the archbishop too had sworn allegiance to Matilda. Henry I had died on 1 December; on 22 December Stephen, not Matilda, was crowned at Westminster.

Stephen surprised and confounded his rivals by the swiftness of his action. He had also won over important allies in England, such as Roger, bishop of Salisbury, and his own brother Henry, bishop of Winchester, who may have been the instigator of the plot; and by the middle of 1136 even such close friends of Matilda as her half-brother Robert, earl of Gloucester, had come over to Stephen's side. If Stephen had governed cautiously and rewarded his friends equally, he might well have managed to obliterate memories of his doubtful claim to the throne. As long as he kept his followers contented, his title would not be questioned; once he disappointed them, the rival claims of Matilda would at once be brought out. There was a further handicap: many of the barons had lands in Normandy, and if Matilda and Geoffrey enforced their rule on the other side of the Channel, such barons would find themselves in a difficult position.

By 1138 both these factors had come into play. Stephen, who relied exclusively on his favorites, Waleran and Robert of Beaumont, had alienated both his brother Henry, by disappointing him of the archbishopric of Canterbury when it fell vacant, and other churchmen, some of whom he had even imprisoned. Meanwhile, Geoffrey was making headway in Normandy, and in June 1138 Robert of Gloucester renounced his allegiance to Stephen and handed over the important towns of Caen and Bayeux to Geoffrey. Within three years Stephen was a prisoner in the hands of his enemies, captured at the battle of Lincoln in 1141.

Matilda's hour had come; but she in turn made the same mistakes as Stephen, compounding them by the proud and arrogant behavior which the barons had feared. It was not the barons, however, who turned decisively against her. The citizens of London, when faced by a demand for a huge sum of money to support her cause, attacked her at Westminster and drove her ignominiously out of the capital before she had been crowned. She had also quarrelled with Henry of Blois, bishop of Winchester, and when she appeared outside that city to bring him to heel, he summoned Stephen's men, who nearly captured Matilda herself. She escaped, but Robert of Gloucester was taken. He was so vital to Matilda's cause that king Stephen was released in exchange.

By the end of 1142, the tables were turned once more, and Matilda was shut up in Oxford, closely besieged by Stephen. Matilda had sent urgent appeals for support to Geoffrey in Normandy. Realising that Matilda was too controversial and difficult a character to be accepted as heir to the throne, he had sent their son Henry with a small army. Henry landed in England for the first time at Wareham in Dorset in November 1142.

Henceforth the Angevin strategy was to place Henry on the English throne. But this did not improve the immediate situation. Matilda extricated herself from Oxford by a daring escape: she was lowered from the walls in a basket and walked through the enemy lines in a white cloak in the depths of a snowy December night. Her supporters were demoralised, and Henry's arrival did not produce any dramatic results: a stalemate followed, with the south-west supporting the Angevins and the rest of the country under Stephen's rule. Henry spent only a few months in England, and then rejoined his father in Normandy, where fortune favored the Angevin cause. Geoffrey had made little progress in his attempts to win the duchy until Stephen's imprisonment in 1141. Thereafter he made swift advances, and by 1145 he was recognised as its duke by the king of France, who was overlord of Normandy, ruling both in his own name and that of Henry.

The barons who held lands on both sides of the Channel were now

Knights erecting a tent during a campaign; from an early 13th century manuscript. (British Museum)

faced by the dilemma which Stephen must have feared from the first, and which finally undermined his cause: in Normandy they owed allegiance to the house of Anjou, in England to the house of Blois. Stephen's cause in Normandy was almost hopeless, while the rival Angevin cause was still very much alive in England.

In 1147 Henry crossed once again to try his luck against Stephen, but his forces, mostly hired soldiers, were too small and badly paid. In one of the oddest episodes of the confused conflict, Henry ended up appealing to Stephen for money to pay off his mercenaries and to go home. This reverse was followed by a yet more serious blow to Henry's cause: the death of Robert of Gloucester in October 1147. Lacking his support, Matilda retired to Normandy in 1148, and it seemed as though England and Normandy would once more go their separate way. A further expedition in 1149 by Henry, on which he was ceremonially knighted by his new-found ally the king of Scotland, met with little better success.

Henry was sixteen when he returned to Normandy early in 1150, and his father now handed over Normandy to him. The reasons for this move are obscure, as Geoffrey appears to have been ruling as duke in his own right, and had done much to re-establish good government there. Both in Anjou and Normandy, Geoffrey had showed an ability for organisation similar to that of his father-in-law, Henry I, and he was to hand on this talent in full measure to his son.

The French king, Louis VII, at first refused to recognise Henry as duke. After a brief and indecisive war in 1151, however, a truce was declared; the count of Anjou and duke of Normandy were to go to the French capital to submit the quarrel to arbitration.

When Henry and his father rode into Paris for the ceremony of investment and homage, it was Henry's first visit to the greatest city in Europe. The French king's court was the most glittering in the western world; Louis VII and his wife, Eleanor of Aquitaine, had just returned from crusade, having achieved an ambition which most other princes dreamt of but never fulfilled. Eleanor herself, at twenty-eight, was the most famous beauty of the age.

Louis had married Eleanor when she was fifteen, in 1137; she had just inherited the great duchy of Aquitaine, which covered most of south-west France, on her father's death. It was a primarily political match, but Louis seems to have been captivated by Eleanor's beauty. However, they were of very different character: Louis became progressively more ascetic and religious, both before his departure on crusade and after his return, until Eleanor is said to have exclaimed: 'I have married a monk, not a king!' She was high-spirited, flirtatious (though not as wanton as her enemies tried to make out), a patron of poets and of the new school of troubadour poetry, to which her grandfather, William IX, had belonged. The troubadours, who made secular love into a religion, were a world away from Louis' devotions, and the marriage was an uneasy one. There had been rumors of indiscretions on Eleanor's part during the crusade, and the couple had separated; equally serious was the fact that Eleanor had only borne Louis two daughters in fourteen years of marriage. Both for political and personal reasons, there was a possibility that the marriage might

*The east window of Poitiers Cathedral was donated by Henry II and Eleanor
of Aquitaine. This detail shows the donors in the act of presenting the window.
(Author's Collection)*

be dissolved. It may be that Henry looked at Eleanor with more than
usual interest because of this: stories were told in later years of how
the queen of France and the handsome young duke had fallen in love
that summer.

The talks between Louis and Geoffrey, presided over by Bernard,
abbot of Clairvaux, began with Geoffrey refusing to compromise. In
particular, he refused to hand over Gerald Berlai, his rebellious vassal
who had given Louis his original excuse to intervene; when Bernard
threatened him with excommunication, he 'prayed that God would
never pardon his sin' and withdrew from the talks. However, possibly
persuaded by Henry, who was anxious to secure peace in Normandy
in order to invade England, Geoffrey soon returned, and in the end
peace was made at the price of conceding the disputed frontier area of
the Vexin in return for Louis' recognition of Henry as duke.

Geoffrey returned to Anjou at the end of the month: it was very
hot, and on the journey he stopped to bathe in a wayside pool near

Le Mans. A week later he was dead of a fever, aged only thirty-nine. Henry, who had gone to Normandy, hastened south to secure Anjou, and for the time all question of intervention in England had to be laid aside. The following spring, Louis formally divorced Eleanor at a council at Beaugency on 21 March, on the grounds that they were related within the degrees prohibited by the Church, and that the marriage was therefore null and void. Louis had already withdrawn his men from Aquitaine, and Eleanor hastened south to the safety of her duchy, eluding two attempts (one by Henry's younger brother Geoffrey) to capture her and marry her. From Poitiers she sent word to Henry, and by Easter agreement had been reached: after rapid preparations they were married at Poitiers on Whit Sunday 1152, in the cathedral to which they later gave a great east window with their own portraits at the foot.

It was a match with much to recommend it from a political point of view, whether Henry and Eleanor were in love or not. Henry's lands bordered on those of Eleanor south of the river Loire, and they were potential rivals: but Henry needed peace in France to make war in England, and Eleanor needed to find a powerful husband quickly to forestall the attentions of less welcome suitors. Like his father, Geoffrey, Henry had married a woman several years older than himself, and of considerable character. In terms of territorial acquisition both were brilliant matches; and Henry's marriage in its earlier years seems to have been genuinely happy, even if Henry's tastes were for law and scholarship rather than poetry. There was an element of defiance about the match, too, which must have appealed to him: Eleanor should have sought Louis' permission to marry, as one of his chief vassals, and she and Henry were related in the same degree as she and Louis had been. But neither the breach of feudal etiquette nor that of Church law were ever challenged.

Henry had been without lands when he was knighted in 1149; he now found himself, three years later, ruler of more than half the French kingdom, and his territory stretched from the Channel to the Spanish border, with claims to lands as far south as the Mediterranean shore. The speed of his rise to fortune had not made him lose sight of his remaining objective, for he was never a man to abandon a project lightly; and as soon as the marriage celebrations were over, he rode north to Normandy, to prepare an invasion of England in response to an appeal from his supporters there, led by earl Reginald of Cornwall.

But Louis was not going to allow Henry's coup to go unchallenged. He refused to recognise him as duke of Aquitaine, and sought help from Stephen, who sent his eldest son Eustace, heir-apparent to the English throne. He also enlisted the aid of Henry, count of Champagne, who was married to Eleanor's eldest daughter and would inherit Aquitaine if Eleanor did not have a son. As well as these, he won the support of Geoffrey, Henry's younger brother, who had two bones to pick with the new count of Anjou: he had succeeded in winning Eleanor where Geoffrey had failed, and, more important, he was withholding lands which Geoffrey seems to have believed quite genuinely that their father had meant for him. These were four vital castles on the borders of Anjou and Poitou, including Chinon, Loudun and Mirebeau. There were also stories that Count Geoffrey had made his executors promise not to bury him until Henry had sworn to obey his will, without Henry's knowing what it contained. When Henry had sworn the oath, protesting that he did so only in order that the funeral could take place, he found that he was to hand over Anjou to Geoffrey in the event of his conquering England. But the story is certainly an invention, designed to justify a later rebellion by Geoffrey in 1156. It would certainly have been in Geoffrey's interest to help Henry to gain England, rather than delay his invasion plans.

This was Henry's first serious campaign. He now had adequate forces at his disposal, as he had not in the escapades in England, and he showed himself an excellent general. The hallmark of his operations was speed, in an age when armies moved very slowly, encumbered by primitive carts and ill-disciplined footsoldiers. He at once led his troops down from Barfleur to the Norman border, and instead of taking up defensive positions, counterattacked into Louis' own territory, following this by an onslaught on Geoffrey's allies. He persuaded the keepers of the disputed castles to hand them over to him, and then successfully besieged Montsoreau, capturing Geoffrey himself and the more important rebels. At this the enemy coalition collapsed; a truce was arranged, and Henry was once more free to plan his invasion of England.

However, his army had been in the field for some months, and time was needed to gather new troops and provisions; knights would only serve for a limited period of time, and even mercenaries were reluctant to undertake prolonged campaigns. So Henry spent the autumn in Aquitaine with Eleanor, making a formal progress round the duchy and trying to secure Eleanor's authority over her notoriously independent vassals. Even the monks could be recalcitrant: at Limoges, Henry demanded as a contribution towards his expenses the tax customarily paid by the great monastery of St Martial to the ruler of Poitou when he visited the town. When it was refused, on the grounds that he was living in a tent outside the town and not in Limoges castle, he ordered in a fury that the outer walls of the town, which the monks had just built at great cost, should be demolished.

Henry's journey to Aquitaine may also have been designed to mask his true intentions. Everyone expected that the war with France would be renewed in the spring, and Henry seemed to have missed his opportunity to invade England during the autumn. But at Christmas he suddenly returned to Normandy, and in early January sailed from Barfleur with a small fleet of thirty-six ships. He landed on the Hampshire or Dorset coast about 6 January; one story tells how he went to a nearby chapel to hear Mass, and as he entered the priest read the opening words of the lesson, 'Behold the Lord our governor, and the kingdom in his hand.' It was as favorable an omen as he could have wished for. No one had expected his arrival; it was blowing a gale in the Channel, and his enemies in France had had no word of his plans. Stephen's son Eustace was still abroad, and only returned when he heard of Henry's crossing.

During the years of Henry's absence, his supporters, heartened by his rising fortune in France, had put up a brave resistance to Stephen's onslaughts. But Stephen's mercenary armies had held them down, and they had been forced to fight a defensive war until such time as Henry could come to their aid. Their base was still southwest England, reaching as far as the castle of Wallingford on the Thames, an isolated outpost in Stephen's territory which Stephen was now besieging. Henry was reluctant to commit himself to trying to raise a siege so far from his main base. Instead, by a shrewd piece of strategy, he drew Stephen away by attacking the equally isolated royalist outpost at Malmesbury. He seized the town, and Stephen arrived while he was besieging the

Norman soldiers defending a castle by hurling rocks at their attackers; from the **Bury St. Edmunds Bible**, *c.1121. (Corpus Christi College, Cambridge)*

castle. The two armies were drawn up outside the town on either bank of the river Avon; Henry had perhaps three thousand men, Stephen slightly more. But Stephen's men were facing into the teeth of a bitter storm, and were soon so numb they could scarcely hold their swords. Neither side was anxious to fight, and a truce was agreed, whereby the fortifications at Malmesbury were to be demolished and the siege at Wallingford was to be raised for six months.

Henry's star was now in the ascendant: the barons had come reluctantly to Stephen's summons, and soon after the truce, Robert, earl of Leicester, changed his allegiance, bringing thirty castles in the Midlands under Henry's control. A prolonged but successful siege at

Tutbury castle brought Earl Ferrers over to his side, and a detachment took Warwick castle. Bedford, Stamford and Nottingham were attacked as well, before Henry returned to the central point of the conflict at Wallingford.

Stephen had built a rival castle at Crowmarsh, just across the river, with the object of hindering access to Wallingford, and was trying to starve out the garrison. Henry attacked this, but was nearly caught in an ambush by Stephen's men. He withdrew and began to gather a large army in Oxfordshire, while Stephen also raised troops. In August the two armies moved towards Wallingford and encamped on either side of the river. Henry seized a bridge which Stephen had barricaded, and a pitched battle seemed imminent. But neither side was prepared to risk such an encounter, and under pressure from his barons, Stephen agreed not only to a truce but to the opening of formal negotiations, with the archbishop of Canterbury and the bishop of Winchester as mediators.

There was no real question of Stephen's surrendering the crown to Henry: his position was far too entrenched, despite Henry's recent successes, for this to be a practical solution. But Henry could easily be declared heir to the kingdom after Stephen's death. The only obstacle to such a plan, favored by a number of Stephen's followers, was Stephen's son Eustace. In 1152, Stephen seems to have tried to obtain permission from the pope to have Eustace crowned as his successor, but the archbishop of Canterbury gave such a bad report of his character that the pope refused to allow the coronation.

Eustace was a typical product of his age, chiefly interested in fighting, pillage and destruction. His only good quality was a dogged courage. As soon as the armies parted, both sides began to try to secure the best possible bargaining position. Eustace, however, went on the rampage in Cambridgeshire and East Anglia, possibly hoping that his excesses would force Henry to engage him in battle. But on 17 August, having ravaged the lands of the great abbey at Bury St Edmunds, he died of a sudden illness, which, so men said, was divine retribution for his misdeeds. On the same day Eleanor bore Henry's first son, William, in Aquitaine.

Even with this obstacle out of the way, the negotiators made slow progress, and it was only on 6 November at Winchester that the peace was finally sealed. The exact terms were announced by Stephen in a charter issued at Westminster at Christmas. Henry had done homage to Stephen, who had declared him to be his son and heir. Stephen's second son, William, was to retain all his existing lands, but, it was implied, had no claim on the throne. Henry's supporters had done homage to Stephen, and the chief castles of the kingdom were to be given to keepers agreed by both parties. Finally, Stephen agreed to take Henry's advice in all matters concerning government, reserving exclusive rights only in questions of justice.

There were still problems, however. Unlawful castles, many belonging to loyal supporters of the two rivals, had to be destroyed; and, as there were reckoned to be over a thousand of these, it was hardly surprising that there were difficulties which at one moment, in January, threatened to lead to a renewed war. There were disputes, too, over rights to land; each side had been prodigal with grants to its supporters, and the rival claims took many months, if not years, to resolve. Henry spent much of the first three months of 1154 in Stephen's company trying to settle these difficulties, before returning to Normandy just before Easter.

There was no immediate likelihood of Henry's succeeding to the English throne. Stephen was only fifty-three, and Henry I had been sixty-seven when he died: even with the shorter expectation of life of the time, Stephen was by no means an old man, and Henry was a mere twenty-one. He was in no hurry to inherit, as he had still much to do in his French domains by way of establishing his authority and securing his position. He spent the summer in Normandy and Aquitaine, and succeeded in making peace with Louis, buying back two towns from him. In September, Henry was seriously ill, and had to rest for a time, but in October he was active again, helping Louis to suppress a revolt on the Norman border. This alliance sounds unlikely in the light of earlier hostilities, but it seems that Henry and Louis liked each other in spite of their political disputes and their own very different characters.

In early November, Henry was back in Normandy, besieging a rebellious vassal at Torigny, when word came from England that Stephen had died of a slight chill at Faversham in Kent on 25 October. Henry took the news calmly; what he had seen in England earlier that year was enough to convince him that he could be sure of his inheritance. He summoned Eleanor from Aquitaine, and while he waited for her he brought the siege at Torigny to a successful conclusion. Accompanied by Henry's brothers Geoffrey and William, they went to Barfleur in mid-November, but were delayed by unfavorable winds until the first week in December, when they set sail.

On 8 December, Henry landed in England for the fourth time. Three times he had come as an invader; now he came to claim his inheritance. 'For almost six weeks England was without a king,' wrote a chronicler, 'but the peace was not disturbed, either for love or fear of the king to come.' England's long anarchy was at an end; on 19 December, Henry and Eleanor were crowned together in Westminster Abbey by archbishop Theobald, according to the ancient ritual of the realm. Henry had realised his grandfather's dream of a united Anglo-Norman state. More than that, as king of England, duke of Normandy and Aquitaine, count of Anjou and Maine, the twenty-one-year-old Henry Plantagenet was the greatest ruler in the western world.

Chapter 2

King of England

*T*he only contemporary portraits of Henry are all formal images of what a king should look like: even the effigy on his tomb is a kind of ritual figure. To find his real image, we have to turn to men who knew him and wrote about him, both friends and enemies. Fortunately three of his courtiers left such pen-portraits, and from them we get a vivid picture.

Henry was of middle height, stocky, well built, and very strong. His face was square, with fiery red hair and beard and freckled complexion. Men compared him to a lion, particularly when he was angry: then his eyes grew bloodshot and his face flushed crimson. Normally, his expression was mild, his eyes large and grey; and although his rages were memorable, they were not frequent. His temperament was cool and calculating, though his moods could change without warning. He was always on horseback, and as he only wore gloves when out hawking and kept his hair close-cropped, he might easily have been mistaken for one of his own servants, had it not been for his impressive manner and bearing. He was handsome, but had no time for the high fashions of some of his followers, preferring practical clothes suited to the outdoor life he led. Ignoring the conventions of the English and Norman barons, who wore long cloaks, he clung to the short Angevin cloak he had worn since boyhood, earning the nickname 'Curtmantle'.

He was unconventional in other ways. He was far more interested in laws and learning than tournaments and troubadours: Peter of Blois, himself a distinguished scholar and churchman, said of him: 'With the

King of England, it is school every day; there is always conversation with learned men and discussion of learned problems.' It was one of his ancestors as count of Anjou who was reputed to have said to the king of France that an uneducated king was no better than a crowned ass; and his father and grandfather had both been interested in the world of scholarship and letters—all the more remarkable in an age when further education was almost exclusively directed towards a career in the Church, and many barons could do little more than read simple documents and sign their own name. Henry had an amazing memory, and could speak—so it was said—every language used from France to the river Jordan. He normally spoke in French and wrote in French or Latin. Like all the Norman lords, he spoke no English, which was regarded as the language of serfs.

His way of life was unconventional as well. He was restless and energetic, for all his calculating temperament. His courtiers' chief complaint was that he had no regard for his own comfort—or for anyone else's, for that matter. He never sat down, except to eat; so the courtiers had to stand as well. He travelled incessantly, so the courtiers had to go with him, and Peter of Blois has left a lively picture of the chaos that the king's habits produced.

> If the king had promised to remain in a place for that day—and especially when he has announced his intention publicly by the mouth of a herald—he is sure to upset all the arrangements by departing early in the morning. As a result, you see men dashing around as if they were mad, beating their packhorses, running their carts into one another—in short, giving a lively imitation of Hell. If, on the other hand, the king orders an early start, he is certain to change his mind, and you can take it for granted that he will sleep until midday. Then you will see the packhorses loaded and waiting, the carts prepared, the courtiers dozing, traders fretting, and everyone grumbling ...When our courtiers had gone ahead almost the whole day's ride, the king would turn aside to some other place where he had, it might be, just a single house with accommodation for himself and no one else. I hardly dare say it, but I believe that in truth he took a delight in seeing what a fix he put us in. After wandering some three or four miles in an unknown wood, and often in the dark, we thought ourselves lucky if we stumbled upon some filthy little hovel. There was often a sharp and bitter argument about a mere

hut, and swords were drawn for possession of a lodging that pigs would have shunned.

The courtiers said that he covered impossible distances, riding as though he was one of his own messengers: but he knew the value of speed in an age when communications were slow, and many of his more dramatic coups were due to his capacity for hard riding. He was rarely out of the saddle for long, as his slightly bowed legs showed, and when he was not riding on business, he was hunting or hawking. Even when he was occupied by affairs of state, he would turn aside to go hawking along the rivers and streams beside his route, as he did on the way to a vital meeting at Northampton in 1166. He was a bold rider when hunting. Starting at crack of dawn he would spend all day in the saddle, regardless of the country he rode across, plunging into the depths of the great royal forests or across moors and mountain ranges.

For all this energy and restlessness, Henry was also approachable and affable, even to those in disfavor. Whether he was arguing with scholars or listening to the throng of suitors who pressed about him whenever he appeared in public, he would hear them out patiently and give them an answer. He knew well enough how to be devious himself, yet he could not abide longwindedness or deviousness in others. He once reduced a bishop to a state of terror during a lawsuit by stopping him in mid-speech and demanding to know the truth of the matter, when the bishop had been making elaborate and dubious claims to land belonging to an abbey. On the other hand, when bishop Hugh of Lincoln came to Henry to be reprimanded for excommunicating one of Henry's officials, he found the king resting in a forest clearing. There was an ominous silence when Hugh came up, and the king ignored him, continuing to stitch up a leather bandage on his finger. Hugh, unabashed, waited for a minute or two, and then remarked—referring to the tradition that William the Conqueror's mother had been a tanner's daughter from Falaise—'How like your cousins of Falaise you are!' Henry laughed uproariously, and Hugh was at once restored to favor.

Henry's weaknesses were his occasional outbursts of fury, one of which was to have serious consequences. Stories were told (by his enemies) of how he rolled on the ground, chewing the rushes strewn on the floor and tearing his clothes when news of treachery was brought to him. Treachery was in fact his obsession: if he suspected a man of being a traitor, or felt that someone had betrayed him, he would pursue him implacably. But he could understand and tolerate open opposition. He was not a particularly good judge of character, however, and sometimes saw treachery where there was none, and trusted opponents who betrayed him. In his passion for order and justice, he sometimes forgot the human element. This mixture of calculation and mistrust stemmed in part from his early years of hardship, in part from his mother Matilda, who was said to have taught him his less pleasant tricks. One of Henry's courtiers says that she told him to treat men like hawks, taming them by alternate gifts and deprivation; and she taught him to make everything dependent on his will, spinning out business if necessary, and holding on for as long as possible to casual royal income, such as the revenues from a bishopric between the death of a bishop and the appointment of his successor. The gentler Angevin ways of the Plantagenets and the ruthlessness of the Normans mingled uneasily in Henry's character.

Such was the young man who now ruled England, an England ravaged by two decades of civil war, where men still lived in the shadow of the dark days described by the writer of the Anglo-Saxon Chronicle, himself one of the oppressed:

> For every powerful man built his castles…and they filled the country full of castles. When the castles were built, they filled them with devils and wicked men. Then, both by night and day, they took those people that they thought had any goods—men and women—and put them in prison and tortured them with indescribable tortures to extort gold and silver; for no martyrs were ever so tortured as they were. They were hung by the thumbs or by the head, and corselets were hung on their feet. Knotted ropes were put round their heads and twisted until they penetrated to the brains. They put them in prisons where there were adders and snakes and toads, and killed them like that. Some they put in a torture chamber—that is in a chest that was short, narrow and shallow, and they put sharp stones in it and pressed the man in it so that he had all his limbs broken. In many of the castles was a 'noose-and-trap'—consisting of chains of such a kind that two or

three men had enough to do to carry one. It was so made that it was fastened to a beam, and they used to put a sharp iron around the man's throat and his neck, so that he could not in any direction either sit or lie or sleep, but had to carry all that iron. Many thousands they killed by starvation …When the wretched people had no more to give, they robbed and burned all the villages, so that you could easily go a whole day's journey and never find anyone occupying a village, nor land tilled. Then corn was dear, and meat and butter and cheese, because there was none in the country. Wretched people died of starvation; some lived by begging for alms, who had once been rich men; some fled the country.

In the last years of Stephen's reign, there had been some progress towards restoring order; and Stephen and Henry in 1153-4 had curbed the worst of the barons' excessive power, destroying their castles and making the king's law felt once again. The machinery of government had survived in working order, and Henry looked back to his grandfather's days for a basis on which to rebuild stable government.

His work in England for the first five years of his reign was all directed to this end. Within three years taxes were being collected normally, except where the land had been so ravaged in the civil wars that there was no one to pay them; the barons, apart from a brief revolt by Hugh Mortimer in 1155, had accepted Henry's authority; and the royal administration was now led by a brilliant young archdeacon from Canterbury, Thomas Becket, who became chancellor within a few months of Henry's coronation. Becket was fourteen years older than Henry, an experienced diplomat and churchman, whose father was a London merchant. Despite their very different backgrounds and temperaments, they became firm friends, and Henry entrusted Becket with much important and difficult business, giving him power to act on his own initiative.

The heart of Henry's lands might be peaceful, but there was always trouble stirring somewhere on the borders. In 1157, Henry led an army into North Wales, in an attempt to settle the intermittent warfare that had gone on along the border ever since the Norman conquest of England. It was not a success. Henry was ambushed by the Welsh under Owain of Gwynedd, and narrowly escaped in the confusion. Norman weapons and tactics were not suited to full-scale campaigns in mountain territory, and Henry quickly withdrew. The following year, he was more successful in South Wales, but in both areas the peace was a fragile one. On the border with Scotland, he managed to regain Westmorland and Cumberland from the new Scottish king, Malcolm, in 1157, by peaceful means: these lands had been the price of Malcolm's father's support for Henry during Stephen's reign.

In Normandy there were also border problems, due to his brother Geoffrey's claims to Anjou and Maine now that he was king of England. It seems that the story about Count Geoffrey's will was put about once Henry had been crowned, but Geoffrey needed Louis' support if he was to make anything of his claim. Henry realised this and carefully placated Louis when negotiations opened in February 1156. Geoffrey attempted to rebel by himself, but Henry reduced his castles one by one. Later in the year, when the citizens of Nantes threw out their count and offered the title to Geoffrey, he was glad to accept, and the rivalry between Henry and his brother was at an end. Geoffrey's career as count was brief, because he died in 1158.

By 1158, Henry had begun to think in terms of recovering the lands he had lost to Louis of France during his struggle to claim his inheritance. The area in question was the so-called Norman Vexin, containing the castles of Gisors, Neauflé and Neufchâtel: Without these castles, the Norman border no longer ran along the natural frontier, the river Epte, and the French held three vital castles on the Norman bank. Henry decided to employ Becket on the negotiations designed to recover these castles, the object being to arrange a match between Henry's eldest surviving son, Henry, and Louis' daughter by his second wife. To underline the power and prestige of the Anglo-Norman kingdom, Becket travelled with an immense retinue:

> He had about two hundred of his own household mounted on horseback, including knights, clerks, stewards, serjeants, squires and sons of nobles bearing arms in his service, and all in fit array. These and all their train were resplendent in new and festive attire, each according to his rank. He himself had four-and-twenty changes of raiment ...many garments of silk—almost all of which were to be given away and left overseas—every kind of fur, miniver and skins, cloaks and carpets, too, like those which customarily adorn the

chamber and bed of a bishop. He had with him hounds and birds of every kind, such as kings and rich men keep.

In his equipage he had also eight waggons, each drawn by five horses, in size and strength like chargers. Each horse had its appointed groom, young and strong, girt in a new tunic and walking beside the waggon, and each waggon had its driver and guard. Two waggons bore nothing but beer, made by a decoction of water from the strength of corn and carried in iron-hooped barrels, to be given to the French, who admire liquor of this sort, for it is certainly a wholesome drink, clear, of the colour of wine and of superior flavour. One waggon was used for the furniture of the chancellor's chapel, one for his chamber, one for his bursary and another for his kitchen. Others carried different kinds of meat and drink, others cushions, bags containing nightgowns, bundles of clothes and baggage. Twelve packhorses and eight chests carried the Chancellor's gold and silver plate, his cups, platters, goblets, pitchers, basins, saltcellars, salvers and dishes. Other coffers and packing-cases contained his money—more than enough for his daily expenses and presents—his clothes, some books and similar articles. One packhorse, in the van of the others, bore the sacred vessels of the chapel and the ornaments and books of the altar. Each packhorse had its own groom fitly provided. Each waggon had a dog chained to it, large, fierce and terrible, capable, it seemed, of subduing a lion or a bear.

The lavish pageant gained its objective, and Becket arranged a draft agreement by which the young Henry was betrothed to Margaret, with the desired dowry. There was apparently no question of the marriage taking place for the moment, as the two children were four and two respectively; but Margaret was to be brought up at the English court. In addition, Henry was granted a free hand to solve the disputes which had arisen in Brittany on his brother's death. When Henry went to Paris later in the year, he travelled very modestly, in sharp contrast to Becket; and the contrast was even more effective than a renewed display of magnificence. When the agreement was sealed, Henry and Louis went off together on a visit to Normandy and the Breton border. As they stayed one night at the great Norman abbey of Bec, one of the monks heard Louis say that he thought more of Henry than anyone else in the world.

He was less enthusiastic a year later, when news came that Henry was trying to enforce, on behalf of Eleanor, the rights of the rulers of Aquitaine to the overlordship of Toulouse. Louis, when he was married to Eleanor, had solved the problem by marrying his sister to the count of Toulouse, and making a close alliance with him. So any attempt to enforce the claim was likely to bring Henry into conflict with Louis. Henry seems to have hoped that Louis might turn a blind eye to the military operation which he was planning, but events proved otherwise. Becket played a large part in the campaign, and a great army left Poitiers in June 1159, chiefly made up of hired soldiers.

Henry first attacked the count's lands, subduing the region on the borders of Aquitaine and Toulouse and taking the city of Cahors, in the hope that the count would surrender. But Henry's attempts to besiege Toulouse faced insuperable obstacles. Firstly, Louis had not only supported the count, but was actually in the city; and while Henry could make war on him without much embarrassment, it would have been a serious breach of feudal etiquette actually to capture his overlord. Secondly, the nearest base for Henry's army was forty miles away, and supply problems developed. Thirdly, the usual outbreak of camp fever developed after a few weeks, and Henry deemed it prudent to retreat. Louis' brothers had tried to create a diversion by a raid into Normandy, and Henry moved swiftly northwards to retaliate, inflicting far more damage on Louis' lands than had been done to his. As a result, a truce was made in December, followed by a treaty the following spring, which effectively restored the status quo. Henry had overreached himself, and the Toulouse expedition proved a costly failure.

However, the treaty of 1160 did give Henry one advantage. The castles in the Vexin which were to be Margaret's dowry were to be handed over to the Knights Templars, to be transferred to Henry if the young Henry and Margaret were married within three years with the church's approval. This effectively neutralised the disputed area; but it had further consequences as well. In the late summer of 1160, Louis' queen, Constance, died; and with unseemly haste Louis married again. His bride was the sister of the count of Blois, king Stephen's niece, and the match revived an old alliance hostile to the Normans. Henry retaliated by arranging for the marriage of Henry and Margaret to be celebrated at once. This he did by making use of a dispute over the succession to the papacy.

The two rival candidates, Alexander III and Victor IV, were canvassing for support; Louis had already recognised Alexander, and his legates were now in Normandy, seeking Henry's recognition. Henry's bargain was simple: he would recognise Alexander if the legates performed the marriage, and on 2 November they did so. The Knights Templars duly handed over the castles, and although Louis led a brief campaign against Henry that autumn, there was little he could do, and peace was made in the summer.

Henry now turned from consolidating the lands he had inherited to strengthening the royal power within those lands. This was to occupy him for the next ten years, and was to bring him into conflict with the other two great powers within his domains, the church and the barons.

His first move is one of the most puzzling of his whole reign. In April 1161, archbishop Theobald of Canterbury died. He had been a staunch supporter of Henry since the later years of the civil war, and he had been Becket's mentor. Henry filled the vacancy by securing Becket's election as archbishop. Although the chancellor was always a high-ranking cleric, the offices of archbishop and chancellor had never before been combined. We do not even know whether the election was Becket's idea or Henry's, though it is generally assumed to have been the king's. Henry may have intended to copy the arrangement in Germany whereby the archbishop of Mainz was also the emperor's chancellor; if so, he may have been acting on his mother's advice, as this was a longstanding tradition in the Empire.

Such a plan would fit in well with Henry's other activities about this time. The church had its own legal system, which functioned in parallel with that of the king. Normally matters ran smoothly enough, but there were always cases which lay on the borderline of the church's and the king's law and rights, and although Henry had managed to avert any conflict in the early years of his reign, it would clearly be a great advantage to him to have a trusted friend as archbishop. But the scheme not only did not work; in due course it proved disastrous.

Professor Warren, in his monumental biography of Henry, suggests another reason why Henry appointed Becket: he considers that Becket's over-enthusiasm on the Toulouse campaign had persuaded him that 'his friend was a man of defective judgement'; so he promoted him out of the circles of power into the archbishopric, a treatment which Becket resented. This ignores one crucial and well-documented episode: Henry's fury when Becket resigned the chancellorship. If this had been Henry's intention, he could scarcely have been angry; and there would have been no reason for even the most ardent supporter of the archbishop to invent such an episode. And if Henry felt that Becket's judgement was poor, he would hardly have entrusted him with such an important office. What is certain is that Henry misread Becket's character; and here we come up against one of Henry's fundamental faults. He might be a good strategist, knowing how to outwit his enemy, but he never seems to have been able to assess the motives of his opponents, as we shall see in his dealings with his sons and with Louis' successor, Philip Augustus. His suspicion and unease, and violent reaction to treachery, all betray an uncertainty about his own judgement of other people.

Henry's mistake was to assume that Becket as archbishop would be the same as Becket as chancellor: easy-going, worldly, knowledgeable about church affairs but prepared to use that knowledge—he had spent ten years as Theobald's close adviser—in Henry's service. In this the king was wrong. Becket's character is still an enigma today, made all the harder to read because we know the outcome of the tragedy. The most convincing assessment is that Becket as chancellor was playing a part; as archbishop, he found his true calling—though cynics would say that he was merely playing a different role. Becket certainly seems to have been an enthusiast, and capable of play-acting at times: witness the great parade of pomp on the embassy to Paris, and his actions on the Toulouse campaign, where he personally led a retinue of seven hundred knights raised at his own expense. But he was always a churchman at heart, as his personal restraint as chancellor shows. He spent lavishly, but only on his household and the outward show of his high office, while remaining frugal himself, and giving away much of his income to charity. If this assessment is correct, his appointment as archbishop meant that his enthusiasm and his underlying bent for church affairs and the holy life now coincided.

However, the change was not immediate, despite Becket's resignation from the chancellorship, Becket threw himself into the work of the archbishopric with his customary zeal, creating a new festival (that of Trinity Sunday) to mark the day of his consecration, and defending the archbishopric's rights over clergy and laymen alike. At first only minor matters came up; but when Becket strayed into the very sphere which Henry had hoped to render harmless by his appointment, the conflicting claims of church and state, the atmosphere quickly became hostile.

He excommunicated a baron with whom he was in dispute without the king's permission, a clear breach of tradition; he demanded homage from the earl of Clare for disputed lands in Kent; and he opposed an apparently harmless financial reform proposed by Henry at a council held at Woodstock in 1163. This was the first sign that real trouble lay ahead. Becket had no real ground for opposing the change, which meant that certain taxes would be paid to the exchequer in London instead of into the coffers of the local sheriff, and his action marks the beginning of his obsession, bordering on mania, with the observance of ancient customs and 'liberties' against the encroachments of royal power. Henry, for his part, was equally determined to see justice done, not merely as an extension of royal power, but as a substantial ideal—he did not argue with scholars for nothing. In the clash of their cherished ideals, the friendship between Becket and Henry was shattered.

Justice lay at the heart of the issue which was to bring the quarrel into the open. Becket could be tolerated as an independent, perhaps slightly eccentric, archbishop, provided that no major issue arose. But there was a long-standing scandal touching both church and state which Henry was determined to put right. It was accepted that anyone in holy orders, from the humblest deacon upwards, was entitled to trial by the church courts, and was exempt from the royal courts. This would have caused no problem had there been a clear means of identifying clerics and an identical scale of punishments. As it was, men often pleaded so-called 'benefit of clergy' when they were not entitled to it; and if they were convicted in the church courts they would only be deprived of their orders. Both sides agreed that there should be no second trial in such cases, but Henry argued that the convict should be handed over to his officers for punishment. This was resisted by Becket and the church on the grounds that the offender would be punished twice for one crime.

In the previous century, clerks had been tried in secular courts for secular offences; and there is no doubt that Becket's position was based

35

on new ideas from the Continent which had been introduced during Stephen's reign when royal power was weak. Becket never claimed that he was defending ancient customs in this case; on the other hand, the weight of opinion within the church was on his side. Henry had a good case in terms of traditional practice, and an even better one in practical terms, because lawless clergymen were all too common and their immunity to royal justice brought the king's courts into disrepute. In 1163, the royal justices gave the king a list of over a hundred murders committed by clerks. But there was no clear cut way out of the dispute, and it degenerated almost at once into a trial of strength.

The king first put his proposals to the bishops at a church council at Westminster in October 1163. Relying on arguments from the church's own laws, he suggested that the correct procedure with 'criminous clerks' was to hand them over to the royal courts for sentence once they were defrocked by the church court, saying that this was the ancient custom of England. The bishops, led by Becket, argued against the king's proposals, and when Henry angrily challenged them to say whether they supported the ancient custom of the kingdom, Becket, acting as their spokesman, said that they did, qualifying the statement with the words 'saving their order'. His meaning was that they supported the customs only when they did not conflict with church laws; and he had just said that in his view the king's proposals did exactly that. Faced with this unexpected and united opposition, Henry withdrew from the council in a fury. He had at least hoped for negotiations, not an obstinate refusal to consider ways of dealing with the problem.

Henry's only way out was to try to break the united front of the bishops, and by the spring he had succeeded in doing so. Three of the bishops, for different reasons, withdrew from the firm stand they had taken: the archbishop of York, an old colleague of Becket's in archbishop Theobald's household; Gilbert Foliot, bishop of London, a remarkable man and in many ways a greater figure than Becket himself, who disliked and distrusted Becket; and the bishop of Chichester, who seems to have hoped to reconcile the two parties. Henry also sent messengers to the pope, Alexander III, who, fearing that Henry might change his allegiance to his rival Victor IV, urged Becket to accept the royal customs without reservations. At the end of the year, Becket made his peace privately with the king at Woodstock; but Henry insisted that his acceptance should be as public as his original refusal. A great council was summoned to meet at Clarendon, near Salisbury, in January 1164.

Henry had more in mind than a merely verbal ceremony. When the bishops arrived, they found that the 'customs' in dispute were now a written text, which they were required to seal. Becket refused to do this, saying that these customs had never been known in England, but were 'pernicious innovations'; and he held out, supported by the bishops, for three days, in the face of the king's blackest anger. Then he suddenly gave way. Gilbert Foliot later claimed that the other bishops had been ready to stand firm, and that Becket was the first to yield, forcing the others to seal the document.

Peace was made for the moment, but the causes of the dispute remained. Becket's sudden change from obstinacy to complete obedience meant that there had been no negotiations when a compromise was urgently needed to avoid future trouble. Henry had made a serious mistake in insisting that the unwritten, ill-defined customs should become written law. He was perhaps looking enviously at the written law studied in the universities, Roman law, and the canon law of the church itself, and trying to imitate it. But his way of thought, that agreements should be written and precise, was alien to English and Norman tradition, and he was an innovator ahead of his time. The written definitions looked much more ominous to bishops and barons alike than the vaguer terms of remembered custom.

Henry immediately sought to obtain papal approval for the written customs, the so-called 'Constitutions of Clarendon.' Becket at once repented that he had sworn to accept them. When the pope refused to agree to the customs, Henry blamed Becket, branding him traitor, and began to look for a way of bringing him down. The original issues were quickly lost in a mere clash of personalities. It no longer mattered whether right and justice were on one side or the other; it was only a question of who would win and who would lose.

The first round of the struggle took place at Northampton in October 1164. Becket was accused of failing to answer a summons to the royal court. The charge was just, even though the case involved was a trumped-up one. Becket had indeed ignored the summons. The sentence was far from just: for this one offence, where a small fine would have been appropriate, he was to forfeit all his goods. Henry then dragged up a series of charges relating to debts from his days as chancellor, insisting on either an answer from Becket or a formal trial. Becket claimed with some justification that he had been formally acquitted of such debts when he became archbishop; but Henry insisted on trying to humiliate him. Becket finally said that he would answer the king the next day, 12 October.

Before he went to face Henry, Becket celebrated mass, substituting for the service for St Wilfred's day that for St Stephen's day, which contained the Introit beginning 'Princes did sit and speak against me'. He then proposed to go to the castle in his full vestments, but was dissuaded by his clerks; however, as he dismounted in the courtyard, he took his cross from the bearer, and carried it himself into the council chamber. Foliot accused him of brandishing it as the king might brandish his sword, but Becket refused to relinquish it. When the bishops had assembled, he turned on them for joining in the judgement on him for failing to answer the king's summons, and forbade them to judge him on any further secular charge. He ended by appealing to the pope on the first case.

All this was reported to Henry, sitting with his barons in an upper room. Henry now lost his temper; Becket had broken his oath of allegiance and his oath at Clarendon at the same time. He demanded immediate judgement on the archbishop; but the bishops begged to be excused, offering instead to send a petition to Rome asking for Becket's deposition. The king agreed, and it was the barons alone who gave sentence. But there had been no trial, and Becket angrily refused to hear Robert of Leicester, the justiciar, when he came to announce the verdict. 'Do you think you can judge me?' he broke in as Leicester began to read the verdict. 'You have no right to do so. Judgement is a sentence pronounced after trial, and I have said nothing in any trial today ...Such as I am, I am your father in God, while you are lords of the king's household, lay lords, secular lords. I will not hear your judgement.' With that, still bearing his cross, he pushed his way out into the courtyard and rode off.

That evening, three of the bishops came to ask permission for Becket to depart. Henry appeared cheerful, and said he would give an answer the next day; but Becket did not wait. Leaving the town that night he was in Flanders three weeks later.

Now that Henry's anger had subsided he proceeded coolly and calmly to play the diplomatic game which might have led him to success had he only begun it earlier. He sent a discreet mission to the papal court to take soundings of opinion, but with instructions not to take any positive action. Henry's messengers arrived before Becket, who chose a very different approach. Proclaiming the wrongs done to the English church by Henry's constitutions, he read them out for all to hear, and then, declaring that his election had been by the king's command and was against church law, resigned his archbishopric, saying that he had been the cause of all the trouble. For once, his sense of the theatrical stood him in good stead; the pope reinstated him as archbishop and proclaimed his support for him.

Everything now depended on the pope's attitude, though that of Louis of France was also important. Louis' position was simple: the arrival of Becket as a refugee to his court gave him an excellent diplomatic weapon, of which he made the most. The pope, still fearing that Henry might transfer allegiance to his rival, was in a more delicate position. But Alexander was a skilled diplomat, and throughout the controversy worked steadily towards reconciling the two parties, curbing the excesses of both while safeguarding his own interests. Henry and Becket both loudly proclaimed their disgust. After a visit by one delegation from the pope, Henry declared 'I hope to God that I never see another cardinal in my life!' while Becket sent thunderous letters to the pope showing him the error of his ways. The breach between king and archbishop seemed irrevocable.

And so, in a sense, it was; left to their own devices, neither Henry nor Becket would have come to terms. It was nothing new for the archbishop of Canterbury to go into exile: at the turn of the eleventh century, Anselm, in dispute with William Rufus and later Henry I, had spent several years abroad. But Anselm and Henry I had not quarrelled personally, and in the end an arrangement was reached which satisfied both sides. During Anselm's absence, Henry I had placed his property and that of the see of Canterbury in the care of Anselm's friends, and given instructions that the archbishop should be well provided for. Henry II showed that his quarrel with Becket was of a different kind.

He gave orders for the seizure of all Becket's property, in accordance with the sentence at Northampton, and treated those of Becket's clerks who had followed him into exile as traitors, making their relatives produce surety for good behavior.

However, there were others who wished to bring about a reconciliation between king and archbishop; the moment was to come when Henry needed the archbishop for his own political reasons, and Becket knew that as an archbishop in exile he would gradually lose influence and importance. Four years after Becket's flight, Henry was anxious—for reasons to which we will return—to have his eldest son crowned, to ensure the succession after his death. But English kings could only be crowned by the archbishop of Canterbury, and it seemed imperative to make peace with Becket for this reason.

In January 1169, king and archbishop met in person for the first time since the summer of 1164, at a conference at Montmirail in Normandy, at which Louis was also present. Mediators were appointed, and at first made little headway with Becket, who insisted on retaining the clause 'saving his order' in any acknowledgement of the disputed customs. At length, however, he realised that the mood of the meeting was against him, and that he was regarded as obstinate and foolish in his persistence. He agreed to drop the offending clause, and a formal ceremony of reconciliation was arranged. But in the meantime, he changed his mind. One of his clerks, Herbert of Bosham, an extremist to whom compromise was hateful, claimed to have reminded him of the difficulties that had followed his unconditional acceptance at Clarendon, as the archbishop was going to the ceremony.

Becket went up to Louis and Henry and knelt before the latter. Henry took his hand and made him rise to his feet. After a brief speech, Becket ended: 'As to everything about which we disagree, my lord king, I throw myself on your mercy and pleasure, in the presence of our lord the King of France and the assembled archbishops, lords and others.' Then he added: 'Saving the honour due to God,' and the gathering dissolved into uproar. Henry abused Becket roundly, and said to Louis: 'That means that if my lord of Canterbury disapproves of something, he will say it is against God's honour, and I shall never be able to handle him.' Louis, who was now anxious for a settlement for his own political reasons, commented sarcastically to Becket, 'My lord, are you trying to be more than a saint?' Becket refused to take back his words, and the conference broke up.

As the months went by, Louis, having secured his peace treaty with Henry, began to support Becket again, and it was the pope who took the initiative in trying to arrange a settlement. Becket, furious with the pope's apparent readiness to compromise, issued excommunications of Henry's supporters, and even threatened the king himself with such a sentence. He also menaced Henry's kingdom with an interdict: all church services would be stopped, and no baptisms, marriages or burials could take place. But the pope refused to confirm Becket's excommunications, and sent two cardinals to try to mediate once more.

Meetings went on at intervals through the summer. At Bur-le-Roi on 1 September a provisional agreement was reached, but foundered on the refusal of the cardinals to go to England to absolve those that Becket had excommunicated. Henry left the meeting declaring: 'Do what you like; I could not care less for you or your excommunications!' Negotiations were resumed the next day, but once more broke down. Henry was reminded that the legates could take action against him, and is reputed to have said: 'I know, I know; they will put an interdict on my lands. But if I can capture the strongest of castles in a day, can't I capture one cleric who puts an interdict on me?' The day after, Henry tried to insist on the inclusion of the clause 'saving the dignity of his kingdom' in his formal offer of peace, echoing Becket's own phrase in the knowledge that it would be unacceptable. Despite renewed talks later in the month, nothing was agreed, and Henry, expecting sanctions against him, took the precaution of closing off the ports and forbidding any messengers from the pope or archbishop to enter the realm; anyone found with letters from them would be liable to severe penalties.

But Henry in turn had gone too far, and the English bishops refused to accept his decrees. Under such pressure, a compromise seemed essential, and at a conference at Montmartre in November, terms were at last agreed. Henry now assented to the withdrawal of the customs to which the archbishop objected. Just as everything was completed, Becket asked Henry for the kiss of peace to ratify the agreement. Henry, claiming that he had once sworn that he would never again give Becket

Coronation of a king, from a drawing after Matthew Paris. (Chetham's Library, Manchester)

the kiss of peace, refused, either because he did not want to make this public gesture of reconciliation or because he had had second thoughts about the pact. Once again the meeting broke up without a solution being reached.

The problem of the coronation of the young Henry had meanwhile been in abeyance. Henry was not prepared to let another year go by without the ceremony being performed, and in the spring of 1170 he devised a way out of his dilemma. After Theobald's death in 1161, Pope Alexander had issued letters to Henry enabling a coronation to be performed by any bishop whom Henry chose. These were in fact intended to cover a possible coronation before a new archbishop had been consecrated, but were not dated or limited in any way. Becket had persuaded the pope to write to the English bishops in 1166, forbidding them to carry out the ceremony, but the letter to Henry himself was never withdrawn. Henry decided to arrange for the archbishop of York to carry out the ceremony, putting word about that he had secured the removal of the prohibition of 1166. As no letters from the pope were reaching England, no one could contradict him; and on 14 June 1170 his son was crowned with all due ceremony at Westminster by the archbishop of York. It was a double insult: to Becket, whose rights at Canterbury had been challenged, and to Louis, because his daughter Margaret was not crowned with her husband.

But it was also a bold stroke which had removed Becket's chief weapon and transformed the situation. Henry, having achieved one of his chief aims, could afford to be generous, and at Fréteval on 22 July he offered the same terms as at Montmartre, including the withdrawal of the customs to which Becket objected. As to the question of the coronation, he appeased Becket by offering to allow him to recrown the young king and Margaret, thus preserving the rights of Canterbury, which Becket had zealously defended since his first days as archbishop. No mention was made of the kiss of peace, and as the meeting ended, he and the king talked alone on horseback for a few moments. He asked the king for permission to proceed against the bishops who had taken part in the coronation, and Henry agreed, on the understanding that the punishment would be a formal sentence rather than a real one. Becket thanked him, dismounted, and knelt before the king; but Henry held his stirrup for him to remount, saying: 'My lord archbishop, let us return to our old friendship, and help each other as best we can, forgetting our hatred completely.' Peace seemed to have been made; but it was only a lull before the storm.

Work at once began on restoring Becket's property and that of Canterbury; but six years' lapse made matters very complex, and progress was slow. The same problems reappeared, and new ones as well. Henry could not very well abandon those who had supported him to Becket's wrath, but the archbishop was bent on punishment of those who had infringed his rights, particularly the bishops. At a further meeting at Amboise in October, Becket publicly demanded the kiss of peace, which Henry still refused, even ordering a requiem mass to be celebrated when Becket appeared in the same church one day, to avoid the kiss of peace which was part of the ordinary service. However, no serious quarrel developed, and Henry proposed to cross to England with the archbishop at the end of the year. But he was detained by a quarrel with Louis over Berry, on the borders of Aquitaine and Louis' domain, which had developed into open war; and Becket crossed in the company of John of Oxford, one of Henry's staunchest supporters in the quarrel, at the end of November.

Even if Henry had made his peace with him, there were many men in England, particularly in Kent, who had reason to fear and dislike the archbishop. He had made matters worse by sending letters, just before he himself crossed, excommunicating the bishops who had taken part in the young king's coronation; both the timing and severity of the sentence showed that Becket was as high-handed and tactless as ever. When he landed, he was met by an armed and hostile mob. The common people, according to his supporters, cheered him; but the barons had no time for him, and the young king refused to allow him to come to Windsor. Furthermore, by excommunicating the archbishop of York, Becket had cast doubts on the validity of the coronation ceremony, and thus aroused Henry's worst fears. Becket declared himself ready to absolve the other two bishops when they asked him to do so, but said that only the pope, who had given permission for the sentences, could absolve the archbishop of York.

All three at once left to find the king, who was at Bures in Normandy; they protested about Becket's action, calling it treasonable, and Henry's mood was made even worse by wild stories that Becket had been cheered through London by the citizens and was riding around at the head of a small army of knights. A council was held at Christmas to discuss ways of dealing with Becket. Henry realised that nothing had altered, and Becket was as willful and unpredictable as ever. Someone exclaimed to him: 'My lord, while Thomas lives you will have no peace, no quiet, no prosperity!' The king flew into a rage. Whether he actually said the words attributed to him—'What idle and miserable men have I promoted in my kingdom, faithless to their lord, who let me be mocked by a low-born clerk,' or even 'Will no one rid me of this turbulent priest?'—is far from certain, but his words and manner were such that four knights of his household slipped away in the darkness and rode to the coast, crossing to England at once by different routes.

As soon as Henry noticed that they had gone, he ordered that both they and Becket should be arrested. But it was too late. The knights

The murder of Thomas Becket in Canterbury Cathedral, 29 December 1170; from the Codex Psalmorum Membranaceus, *c. 1190-1200, probably the earliest representation of the scene to have survived. (British Library)*

gathered at Saltwood castle, which belonged to Ranulf de Broc, who had been in charge of the Canterbury lands during Becket's exile, and was the archbishop's sworn enemy. At no point do they seem to have formulated a clear plan, and none of them was other than a simple fighting man. They went to Canterbury on the afternoon of 29 December and confronted the archbishop while he was dealing with official business after dinner. One of them, Reginald FitzUrse, demanded that the archbishop should come with them to the king and go into exile at once, calling him a traitor and breaker of the peace.

It was an incoherent speech, from a man not used to argument and understanding little of the deeper issues at stake. Becket replied calmly, dismissing both threats and demands. At a loss what to do next, the knights retreated, ordering the bystanders to 'take this fellow into custody so that he does not escape'. Becket went down into the cathedral for vespers, while the knights and their followers gathered, undecided, outside the door. They were still unclear as to what to do. They were principally anxious to remove the archbishop as a prisoner, but it was clear that force would have to be used. So they armed themselves, and entered the church; Becket had given orders that the doors were not to be barred, and refused to take any opportunity of escape. The knights had no difficulty in finding him. He once more refused to go with them, and they tried to drag him out of the church. One of them drew his sword and struck him with the flat of the blade, and Becket struggled to resist them. A bystander tried to intervene, and was wounded in the arm; and then Becket himself was wounded. The knights struck out blindly, and Becket fell dying under their blows.

Becket had half-expected, half-invited martyrdom. He knew that there were violent men who hated him, and was prepared to face them rather than seek safety. If FitzUrse and his companions had not taken the initiative, many others were ready to do so. But for Henry his death was a disaster. Two days later a messenger rode up to the castle at Argentan in Normandy. He did not ask to see the king, but told the courtiers the dreaded news that the knights had done their worst and that Becket was dead. At first no one dared to tell Henry; in the end someone, probably one of the chief barons, told the king. Violent grief replaced violent anger. Henry shut himself up for three days, weeping and refusing to eat, until his friends feared for his sanity. Henry mourned his friend of days gone by; but he also feared the future and the blame that would be fastened on him for his rash words.

Becket was at once hailed as a martyr, and Louis and the pope expressed their conviction that Henry was responsible for his death. But the blow that might have been expected never fell. It was true that an interdict was placed on Henry's lands in France, but an English embassy to Rome averted the threatened excommunication of Henry on Maundy Thursday by assuring the pope that the king had played no direct part in the murder. Papal legates were sent to investigate, and by the time they reached France in August, Henry had departed first to England and then to Ireland. The pope was likely to take drastic action only while the memory of the murder was fresh in men's minds; and Henry was playing for time.

When Henry returned from Ireland, where no papal messenger was able to reach him, it was April 1172, fifteen months since the death of Becket. Negotiations with the papal legates began on 17 May at Savigny; terms were quickly arranged, and on 21 May the public ceremony of exculpation and penance was carried out. Henry swore on the Gospels that he had neither ordered nor desired the murder of the archbishop of Canterbury, and that the news had caused him more sorrow than joy. Here he departed from the prepared text, and exclaimed that neither his father's nor his mother's death had caused him such grief. He declared that he would carry out such penance as the legates decreed because his angry words might have led unintentionally to Becket's death.

The legates then read out the terms of the penance and agreement: the bishops were to be released from their oath to observe the Constitutions of Clarendon, the possessions of Canterbury were to be restored, and Henry was to send 200 knights at his own expense to the Holy Land. In return, the pope agreed that the crown had a right to protect its interests if church law or administration came into conflict with royal powers. It was a practical solution, tactfully vague; if Henry had retreated from his earlier attempts to lay down hard and fast lines between Church and state, he still found himself able to maneuver in a way that would have been impossible had Becket still been alive. For the rest of his reign, relations between church and state were harmonious: outstanding disputes were settled amicably. Whatever Becket's merits, he had been the one obstacle to such harmony. While Henry and Becket were both alive, they could see the issues only in terms of victory or defeat. With Becket gone, Henry neither won nor lost.

Chapter 3

The Devil's Brood

No sooner had the quarrel with Becket and its repercussions come to an end than Henry was faced by a new threat to his authority. This time it came from within his own family. Eleanor had borne him five sons and three daughters: the eldest, William, had died in infancy, but Henry, called 'the young king' because he had already been crowned in 1170, was now seventeen. Richard and Geoffrey were fifteen and thirteen respectively; John, the youngest, was only four. In an age when men matured early and were old at forty, the young king was old enough to play a part in the political scene, just as Henry himself had done from an even earlier age. But there were no inheritances to conquer, no great campaigns to be planned, and the young king was ambitious and restless.

His ambitions had been fired by Louis, because the French king was anxious to see his daughter Margaret established as queen of England. During the intermittent warfare in 1167-70, which had accompanied the quarrel with Becket, one of Louis' principal aims had been to get Henry to agree to a division of his lands on his death which would replace the empire controlled by Henry personally by a kind of loose federation ruled by his sons. The coronation of the young king in 1170 had been part of that scheme, by which the young king was to have Normandy and Anjou as well; Richard was to receive Poitou and Geoffrey would become duke of Brittany. No provision was made for John, who was too young to be considered in an age when infant mortality was very high.

It was this last point which proved to be the stumbling block (and which also gave John his nickname of 'Lackland'). In 1173, Henry tried to arrange a match between John and the daughter of the count of Maurienne in south-east France. The count, although in favor of the match, raised the question of John's prospects: he had no share in his father's domains. Henry replied by offering to give him the castles of Loudun, Mirebeau and Chinon, the very castles over which he and his brother Geoffrey had fallen out twenty years before. This time it was the young king who objected: he was impatient for real power, and, encouraged by Louis, had demanded to be given either England, Normandy or Anjou to rule in his own right. He saw this as an opportunity to force his father into a concession, because the gift to John would have to be confirmed by him if it was to be valid. But Henry was too skillful a negotiator for him: the count of Maurienne accepted Henry's assurance that John would get the castles, and the match was settled.

The young king's intervention was a warning to Henry, and he decided to take action. He thought first of putting his son into custody, but finally determined to remove various members of his entourage whom he suspected of fueling the fires of ambition. Several of the young king's close friends were ordered to leave his company. But the young king reacted at once: when the decision was enforced, at Chinon in March 1173, he made his escape from the castle, and within two days was at the French court, where his father-in-law welcomed him with open arms. Louis had probably hoped for some such outcome when he insisted on the young king's coronation. Knowing that Henry would be loath to part with any real power, Louis had calculated that the young king's position, as a king in name only, would quickly become intolerable, and he was ready to lend his hand to anything that would weaken Henry's over-mighty position in France.

There were others, too, who were interested in undermining Henry's authority, barons who had profited from the lawlessness of Stephen's reign or from the lax rule of the dukes of Aquitaine. As a contemporary chronicler in England wrote:

> These men, whom the king had condemned to lose lands for good
> and just reasons, joined his son's party. This was not because they

thought the young king had the better case, but simply because his father, in trying to strengthen the power of the crown, had humbled their pride and demolished or seized their illicit castles. He had ordered men who had seized royal property to be content with their own inheritance, and had forced them to part with such lands; he had sent traitors into exile, executed robbers, hung thieves, and fined men who oppressed the poor.

The young king's plans, however, would have come to little if he had relied only on such discontent, because Henry's authority was still formidable. With Louis' backing it was a different matter. Louis was the guiding spirit behind the first stages of the quarrel, which quickly became a rebellion when the young king rejected his father's offers of conciliation. At a formal court held in Paris, the young king bought the support of the French magnates by offering them grants of land in England. Among them were such old rivals of his father as Theobald of Blois and Matthew of Boulogne, Stephen's nephew and son-in-law. Only one English name figured prominently, that of Hugh Bigod, earl of Norfolk, but three other earls soon joined him: Robert, earl of Leicester, Hugh, earl of Chester and William, earl of Derby. This was a formidable coalition that stretched across the whole of the heart of England. The Scottish king, William, nicknamed 'the Lion,' also offered his support in return for concessions on the border.

Henry knew that beside these there were many others who would join the young king as soon as they felt that the tide of affairs was moving against him. His exactions in Normandy had been just as heavy as in England: in 1171 he had held an inquest into lands unjustly seized from the crown since 1135, and, says a local chronicler, 'by this means he doubled his income'. Higher taxes, more interference by central authority: it was an invitation to rebellion. Henry knew that his cause would be difficult to defend, and instead of rushing into his usual hectic activity, he remained quiet for long periods, hoping to lure his enemies into hasty and ill-considered attempts to rouse him. But the first news to come in after the young king's flight was both unexpected and unwelcome: both Richard and Geoffrey had also fled to the French court, and Eleanor, disguised as a man, had attempted to join them, but had been detained by Henry's men. She was at once put into close custody.

Eleanor's part in the rebellion is difficult to make out. She had no particular reason to support the young king, and there is clear evidence that Richard was her favorite. Richard had been formally installed as duke of Aquitaine at Poitiers in June 1172, in the church of St Hilaire, where he was invested with the sacred lance and banner of Aquitaine by the archbishop of Bordeaux. At a further ceremony at Limoges, the ring of St Valerie was placed on his finger, and he was proclaimed as the new duke. This had been done as part of the arrangements made in 1169 for the division of Henry's lands, and the chronicle of Limoges records that it was at his mother's wish. Having achieved her object, what else did Eleanor want? She seems to have inspired Richard and Geoffrey to go over to the young king's side, and there has been much conjecture about relations between her and Henry.

Most of this conjecture has centered on the difference in their ages: Eleanor was fifty-one, Henry forty, and there were stories of Henry's affairs and mistresses. It was not in the least unusual for a king to have mistresses, and Henry had fewer illegitimate children than many other medieval kings. Two of them were almost certainly born before he married Eleanor. His affair with his most famous mistress, Rosamund Clifford, may possibly have begun about this time, and Gerald of Wales, who was openly hostile to Henry, suggests that Eleanor's jealousy may have been behind her behavior. Henry certainly accorded Rosamund the kind of adoration which he never gave to Eleanor, if we are to believe the stories of the elaborate shrine with silk hangings built above her tomb at Godstow nunnery after her death in 1176. Gerald of Wales is a far from reliable witness, but there is something about his insinuations which rings true. If Henry did indeed take a mistress publicly at this period, it must have been a blow to Eleanor's pride after the years as the acknowledged beauty of the western world and lodestone of the poets. Her attempts at escape led only to close confinement first at Chinon, then at different castles in southern England, for the next decade.

Eleanor is a powerful but shadowy figure, and there are no vivid pen-portraits of her such as there are of Henry. She is in many ways the archetypal lady of the world of courtly love, always accustomed to adulation. Louis had worshipped her, and had been most reluctant to divorce her. She had created a sensation when she went to Palestine with him on crusade (and something of a scandal as well). German students—perhaps from the great university at Paris—sang of her:

If all the world were mine
From sea-coast to the Rhine
I'd gladly lose them all
To have the queen of England
Lying in my arms.

(British Library)

The troubadours of Aquitaine had paid court to her in subtler verses, and her entourage had become the focus of the new intellectual fashions centered on courtly love. One of the greatest troubadours, Bernart de Ventadour, addressed poems to Eleanor, and a later, more down-to-earth age turned him into her lover, misunderstanding the poet's ideals. He followed her to England, but found both the climate and the company uncongenial. Eleanor in her later years probably came to feel the same way about Henry and his court, and from 1168 onwards she spent an increasing amount of time in Aquitaine.

Here in her native land she was at ease. Instead of Henry's court of administrators, practical, busy men with time only to argue some political or legal point—'school every day,' Peter of Blois had said—she could rule in her own fashion and still have time for debates on courtly love, the new ideas based dimly on Arabic and Platonic philosophy that proclaimed that the lover and his mistress were the most important beings in the universe. In its highest form, the lover worshipped his mistress from afar, deriving from her image all his qualities of mind and heart, valor, generosity, and skill in love. Bernart de Ventadour's poems are in this vein, but troubadour poetry as a whole had a very wide range. Eleanor's grandfather, himself one of the first troubadours, had written songs fit only to be bawled by drunken knights after a feast, enigmatic riddle poems, and more orthodox love poems: Bertran de Born, contemporary of Eleanor's sons, taunted them in political satires: while later troubadours lost themselves in the maze of *trobar ric*, where elaborate language finally yielded to deliberate obscurity.

The troubadour movement was a great flowering of secular culture, and Eleanor became one of its goddesses.

But it was a very literary and unreal culture, and this is part of the reason why we know so little about Eleanor's character. Henry's down-to-earth court had men in it who wrote plain descriptions of their king; in Eleanor's everything was transformed into literary conventions, so that two centuries later she was remembered as having sat in judgement in formal 'courts of love', which never existed except in a poet's imagination. Records of her acts, too, are relatively few; but on the slender evidence that survives, her part in the rebellion of 1172 is by no means out of character. Eleanor was duchess of Aquitaine in her own right, and she was as much a born ruler as Henry: in her old age she was to play a far greater part in Richard's reign than in her husband's, when she only appears as mother of his children and, briefly, as his deputy in Aquitaine before the rebellion.

So we come back to the central cause of the revolt: Henry's insistence on retaining real power in his own lands. Henry was entirely justified in doing so as far as his sons were concerned: the young king was charming, handsome and delightful company, but the business of government bored him, and he was chiefly interested in the pomp and circumstance of his position—and in obtaining sufficient revenue to keep up a lavish court. Here Henry and his son differed completely in temperament. Henry was frugal and simple in his tastes, and had no time for the outward trappings of kingship. As long ago as 1157, he had sworn never to wear his crown in public again. He could not understand the young king's desire to squander the revenues he had built up at the cost of such effort and enmity; and it seems likely that Eleanor, too, was not treated as lavishly as she would have liked. In following his mother Matilda's advice, to keep men hungry and obedient, Henry had failed to distinguish between hunger for power, which affected him closely, and hunger for money, which he could easily have afforded.

There were rumors of action everywhere in Henry's domains, but as he waited at Rouen, little real news came in until May. Even then, only minor skirmishes on the Norman border occurred, and Henry made no move until July, when the enemy strategy became clear. A two-pronged attack was mounted on Normandy from the east and south. Even then, Henry made a brief visit to England and on his return continued to await his chance. The eastern attack was led by Philip, count of Flanders, and the count of Boulogne, who was Philip's brother and heir. As they were besieging a castle in north-eastern Normandy, at Driencourt, the count of Boulogne was wounded by a crossbow bolt, and died from his injuries. Full of grief, Philip called off his attack, and Henry at once went into action against Louis, who had come up to Verneuil; the castle there was on the point of surrendering after a siege lasting some weeks. A three-day truce had been arranged, at the end of which the castle would be handed over if no relief force appeared. Henry arrived on the third day, and Louis beat a hasty retreat: many of his men were killed when Henry's men attacked his rearguard.

Henry then turned to deal with an invasion from Brittany. The Bretons knew he was fully occupied in the south of the duchy, and were taken completely by surprise when he moved his army from Rouen to the western border in two days. Their leaders surrendered immediately. By the end of August the warfare on the Continent was at an end, apart from minor disturbances in Aquitaine, and talks were held at Gisors at the end of September to see if a settlement could be reached. Henry's offers were financially very generous, as if he had realised his earlier mistake. But the young king was not yet ready to agree to terms even if he was to have half the English revenues, because his supporters were about to launch an invasion of England.

Robert, earl of Leicester landed at the mouth of the Deben in Suffolk on 29 September. He was joined by Hugh Bigod, earl of Norfolk and the greatest magnate in East Anglia, but his Flemish mercenaries damaged Bigod's lands near Framlingham, and Leicester had to move on alone towards the Midlands, to face an army raised by Richard de Lucy, Henry's chief justiciar. Humphrey de Bohun and the earls of Cornwall, Gloucester and Arundel were the other commanders.

They intercepted Leicester just outside Bury St Edmunds, and de Lucy's cavalry shattered Leicester's smaller contingent of knights. The Flemish mercenaries, who had marched along singing 'Hop, hop, Willikin, England is yours and mine', were mown down by the cavalry once the knights were defeated, and they scattered across the countryside to be slaughtered by the local people wielding scythes and

Orford. (British Tourist Authority)

pitchforks. The earl and his knights were captured, and Bigod quickly sought a truce. Truces were likewise arranged with France and Scotland, and there was no more fighting that year.

Henry remained on the defensive at the beginning of 1174, and the first action was on the Scottish front, where William invaded England, attacking the border castles. At first he met with some success, but an army was raised by the northern lords, who hated the Scots more than they feared Henry. It assembled in Yorkshire in early July and moved slowly north, making such slow progress that on 12 July the leaders of the expedition decided to ride on ahead to reconnoitre, taking a band of some four hundred mounted knights with them A sudden mist descended as they approached William's army, encamped before Alnwick Castle. After wandering helplessly all night, they found themselves only a short distance from the Scottish camp when the mist lifted at dawn. Charging swiftly into the camp, they killed or captured the unprepared Scottish nobles. William himself was taken prisoner after his horse was killed under him. The rest of the Scottish army fled, and the Scottish king was taken to Newcastle for safe keeping.

That same dawn broke on the kneeling figure of Henry before Becket's tomb in the crypt of Canterbury Cathedral. He had spent the night in prayer and fasting, after the monks had scourged him as a penance. Henry had arrived in England only three days before, crossing in the teeth of a gale in order to arrive before the young king, who was planning to invade from Flanders. He went at once to Canterbury, to do penance and to show that his regard for the newly canonised St Thomas was as high as that of the rebels. It was an uncharacteristic gesture; but, coupled with the dramatic news from Alnwick, it prevented the rebels from associating the memory of Becket with their cause. A month later the rebellion in England was at an end: Bigod, Leicester and the other rebels had made their peace before some new disaster overwhelmed them.

Louis had taken advantage of Henry's absence to strike deep into Normandy, and, with the young king, was besieging Rouen. He was unable to put a complete blockade on the town, and the citizens still held one bridge over the Seine by which supplies were reaching them. He attempted to surprise the town during a truce declared for St Lawrence's day, 10 August; but the citizens, who were taking advantage of the truce to hold a tournament outside the walls, were summoned back by a monk, who noticed warlike movements in the French camp and rang the great bell of the church to warn them. Louis' men were driven off; the next day, Henry appeared before the walls after one of his lightning journeys across the Channel, and on 14 August Louis retreated post-haste to French territory, his rear guard harried by Henry's troops. A truce was agreed on 8 September; during the following weeks, Henry led a brief campaign against Richard in Poitou, who, abandoned by his allies, quickly made peace.

When the kings met again at Montlouis on 29 September, it was less to negotiate than to hear Henry announce the terms on which he would receive back the rebels. Henry was rarely vindictive, and he badly wanted peace. His offer was simple: everything was to return to the status fifteen days 'before his sons withdrew from him.'

None of the young king's grants made in Paris were to take effect,

Knights riding to a tournament. (British Library)

and his alliance with Louis was to be dissolved. But his son's grievances had to be met: and, in return for the young king's agreement that John should be given a grant of lands and revenue from England, Normandy or Anjou, Henry offered him immediately two castles in Normandy and £15,000 a year. Richard was given two castles in Poitou, and half the revenues of the country; Geoffrey got half the revenues of Brittany.

Only those whom Henry held prisoner were less fortunate. Eleanor spent the next decade in captivity, mainly at Winchester. It was not a particularly strict confinement, but she was watched and guarded, as if Henry feared her more than his sons. But it was not fear so much as Eleanor's lack of any political power that enabled Henry to hold her captive. He had to come to terms with his sons because they represented the future; Eleanor had played her part in his plans, and belonged to the past. William of Scotland bought his freedom at the price of becoming Henry's vassal, while the earls of Chester and Leicester remained in prison for another three years.

But the peace was a fragile one. Early in 1175, Henry summoned the young king to come to England with him. There was such distrust between father and son that the young king was persuaded by his cronies that Henry intended to imprison him once they set foot in England, and refused to come. Henry managed to placate him, and in a melodramatic scene at Bur-le-Roi on 1 April, the young king, weeping and protesting that he was loyal, repeated his homage to his father. Father and son spent most of the next year together, but by March

Mounted knights in combat attack each other with spears; from a capital of the palace at Estella in Spain. (Foto Mas)

1176, the young king was sufficiently weary of the business of government to ask permission to go on pilgrimage to Santiago de Compostela, the shrine of St James in north-west Spain, which was one of the great focal points for medieval pilgrims. Henry was reluctant to let him stray so far afield but agreed that he could go to Normandy.

He was unable to cross before Easter, by which time his brothers had come over to England. Richard had arrived to discuss with his father a revolt which had broken out in Poitou, headed by the lord of Angoulême. Henry at once saw a means of occupying the young king, and sent him south to help Richard. However, as soon as the rebellion was crushed, the young king began to make friends with his father's enemies and to gather his old associates around him. When the young king's vice-chancellor tried to report this to Henry, he was discovered and sentenced to death as a traitor by his master, and the bishop of Poitiers had to intervene to save him. Instead, he was flogged naked through the streets of Poitiers.

After this episode the young king left Richard, and spent the next three years indulging in the new and fashionable sport of tournaments, at the head of a band of like-minded friends. The young king was an ideal leader for this kind of society: handsome, charming, wealthy and free-spending, he found himself among men who had no real function in the social hierarchy except to wait for the day when they would come into their inheritance. They were called *iuvenes*, youths: but in fact they might be of any age from early teens to mid-forties, and some men spent thirty years in this kind of limbo as knights errant. Their world was another, cruder version of the troubadour courts of the south: they had taken over some of the troubadour ideals, particularly valor and generosity; but they preferred to listen to simple ballads rather than the troubadours' often complex poetry. Valor all too often became mere brawn, and generosity degenerated into spendthriftness. At a notorious festival near Limoges in 1177

> ...the count of Toulouse gave a knight, one Raymond Dagout, a hundred thousand shillings, which he immediately divided into a hundred times a thousand and gave a hundred knights each a thousand shillings. Bertrand Raiembaus had twelve yoke of oxen plough the streets of the castle and sowed them with thirty thousand shillings. William Grose from Martel, who had three hundred knights with him (there were about ten thousand knights at that court), had all their food cooked in the kitchen with wax candles and torches. The countess Sorgest sent a crown valued at 40,000 shillings; they appointed William Mita king of the minstrels. Raymond of Venoul had thirty horses burnt there in front of everyone for a boast.

The young king was at least kept occupied and out of mischief by his passion for tournaments. He had as his tutor-in-arms one of the most remarkable men of the age, William Marshal, who had begun life as a penniless squire. He had distinguished himself in Eleanor's entourage in Poitou in 1168, when the earl of Salisbury was killed in a skirmish with rebels. He was captured, but Eleanor ransomed him, and not long after he was attached to the young king and became the leader of his household knights. We know a good deal about his career with the young king and their success in tournaments, because he commissioned a long biographical poem about himself in his old age. A twelfth-century tournament was a miniature battle, with very few rules. There was no question of individual jousts between two knights before an admiring throng of ladies. The whole affair was a general mêlée often ranging over a wide area of countryside, and rules were of the simplest.

Two or more teams of knights would meet at an agreed place, and perhaps after a song from the attendant minstrels, the tournament would start with a general charge, followed by a series of hand-to-hand combats. Small areas were designated as refuges, for injured knights or knights whose armor needed repair, but there were no boundaries—on one occasion the young king's men pursued their opponents right into a nearby town. The weapons were supposed to be blunted, to avoid serious or fatal injury, but the armour used was normal battle-armor. In French tournaments, squires were only allowed to take part to help their masters if they needed a fresh horse or had lost weapons or parts of their armor; in Germany, some tournaments became real roughhouses, with gangs of foot soldiers taking part and trying to capture knights on their master's behalf. Only in the next century did the much more formal arrangements begin to develop, including the individual jousts. In these early tournaments, there were sometimes as many as a thousand participants, and military tactics were ofen as important as individual prowess.

William Marshal was a strong and skilled fighter, and as any knight who was captured either lost his horse and armor or paid a ransom, he managed to make a small fortune out of the sport during these years. On several occasions, he rescued the young king, who was suitably grateful. But William also acted as a restraining influence, and this and his prowess were eventually to arouse jealousy among the young king's other followers.

From the end of the great rebellion in 1174, there were eight years of relative peace in Henry's empire. There were always local disputes and difficulties, particularly in Aquitaine; there Richard was hard put to it to contain his rebellious barons, who disliked his attempts to impose a strong ducal authority. There was a protracted argument with Louis over rights in the county of Berry, in the heart of France, which was a strategically important border area; but this was solved in a peaceable fashion. In England, Henry was able to pursue the work of revising the system of royal justice and making it more effective.

Other rulers watched him with admiration and envy, and the English court was constantly visited by embassies from overseas. The island kingdom that a century before had hardly counted in European affairs seemed to have become the center of the Christian world. Envoys from Castile and Navarre came to ask Henry to arbitrate between their kings: the proceedings had to be conducted in writing, as Latin spoken with a Spanish accent could not be understood by Henry's court, and French Latin was equally difficult for the Spaniards. Ambassadors came from the king of Sicily, William II, seeking the hand of Joanna, Henry's younger daughter, in marriage: her elder sister Matilda had married a German prince, Henry of Saxony, in 1166. The count of Flanders asked Henry to go on crusade with him. The Greek emperor, Manuel Comnenus, sent an embassy to ask for military assistance against the Turks, writing to Henry as 'his most dear friend.' Frederick Barbarossa, the German emperor, also sought help following his defeat at Legnano in Italy in 1176. Henry sent most of the embassies away with fine words. He was reluctant to involve himself in affairs at the other end of Europe, even though prospects at home seemed fair. Manuel Comnenus was sent a gift of hounds, but no men at arms.

In the autumn of 1179, events in France began to occupy Henry's attention again. His relations with Louis had always been relatively good: Louis, although quick to defend his rights and therefore often at loggerheads with Henry, was easygoing and prepared to accept Henry's vast empire as a fact of life. His sporadic attempts to disrupt the Angevin power died away after the rebellion of 1174, when Henry had shown that he was more than a match for Louis, even with all his own sons ranged against him.

Like Henry, Louis was anxious to secure a peaceful succession in France, and his son, Philip Augustus, was now fourteen. He had planned to have him crowned in August, but shortly before the day fixed for the coronation, Philip had lost his way out hunting, and, wandering all night in the frost, had caught a chill which soon became a violent and dangerous fever. Louis decided to go on pilgrimage to the shrine of St Thomas at Canterbury, and arrived at Dover on 22 August. Henry met him, and a magnificent procession headed by the two kings made its way to Canterbury, where Henry and Louis knelt together at Becket's shrine. Louis made rich offerings, and left again for France after a visit lasting only five days. It was the last time Henry and Louis were to meet; for Louis, returning home to find that Philip had recovered, was himself the victim of a stroke on the journey back. Philip Augustus was crowned on 1 November, and at once became the effective ruler of France, for although his father survived until the following September, he never recovered sufficiently to play a part in the government of France.

At first the new reign in France augured well for Henry. The peace treaties made with Louis were duly confirmed, and when Philip was beset by quarrels between his close advisers and his family, it was Henry who intervened. Only the Flemish count was dissatisfied. Having been the young king's rival in tournaments in the 1170s, and indeed in a great tournament after Philip's coronation, the count turned to serious politics at the end of that decade. He tried to gain influence over Philip, and it was this that had led to the quarrels among Philip's court. In 1181 he was still causing trouble, and Henry's three sons helped the king of France to bring him to submission in a brief winter campaign.

At the beginning of 1182 Henry made his will. He was in good health, not quite fifty, and with no apparent reason to fear the future, yet this moment marks the turning point of his career. After 1182 his activities in affairs of law and government become noticeably less, as though he had completed the structure of administrative and legal machinery that had been so long in the making. Indeed, as Richard's reign was to show, he had built a system that was capable of functioning more than adequately without the king's personal intervention. The routines of government no longer needed his attention; an elaborate system of cross-checks ensured that officials did not become over-powerful; and the revenues were collected regularly and efficiently.

This year also marked the beginning of a series of political reverses for Henry. At the year's end, Henry and his sons assembled for Christmas at Caen. The young king, who had recently dismissed William Marshal because of unproven charges that he had tried to seduce queen Margaret, was in a restless mood again, and increasingly under the influence of Philip Augustus, who fostered his discontent. Henry attempted to appease his eldest son by making Richard and Geoffrey do homage to him for their lands, something which he had previously avoided. Geoffrey agreed, but Richard refused, because the young king claimed that Richard had built a castle at Clairvaux, on the borders of Poitou and Anjou, on land belonging to him. Henry was unable to persuade him, and Richard fled to Poitou, putting his castles in readiness for war.

What followed is very obscure. The young king and Geoffrey were sent to Aquitaine, either to arrange terms with Richard, or to bring him forcibly to heel; but the next positive fact that emerges is that Henry came hurriedly south and besieged the young king, who had shut himself up in Limoges, throwing up a hasty fortification round the town, while Geoffrey summoned mercenaries from Brittany. Whatever had happened in the interval, it was clear that the young king had taken the opportunity to raise the banner of rebellion once again, relying on Richard's unpopularity to win him support in Aquitaine. One of the troubadours, Bertran de Born, had written a satire (or *sirventes*) on the situation which, although not quite right in its details, gives a local view of the characters involved:

> *A new* sirventes, *singer! Music ho!*
> *I'll cry abroad the young king's latest deed:*
> *His father ordered him to quit at once*
> *His claim against his brother Richard's lands,*
> *and he obeyed him!*
> *Henry, landless king,*
> *For it I crown you king of cowards!*
>
> *A coward surely, now you live like this*
> *On paid and promised money; not the peer*
> *Of heroes such as fought in other years.*
> *And, men of Poitou, he betrays your trust;*
> *He lies to you and leaves you penniless.*
>
> *Sir Richard may not want my good advice;*
> *But, heed it or not, I'll tell him this:*
> *Although your brother is no threat to you,*
> *You ought to treat your loyal liegemen well,*
> *And stop the pillage of their lands and crops,*
> *Don't take their castles on the least excuse!*

And then, for all I care, the younger king
Can stay and joust at Flemish tournaments!
If only Geoffrey, noble duke of Brittany,
Had been the eldest of the English princes;
For he's a better ruler than you both!

Geoffrey in fact seems to have been the prime mover in the conspiracy: he supplied the men and did most of the fighting for his brother. Bertran de Born, like most of the barons of Aquitaine, regarded war as the only worthwhile way of making a living, and was ready to applaud anyone who broke the peace, particularly the peace of Richard's stern government. Geoffrey's motives are obscure. He was a schemer, and even Henry's enemies have nothing good to say of him: 'able to corrupt two kingdoms with his tongue', 'that son of perdition.'

The first months of the campaign were difficult for Henry; for once he was not prepared, and it took time to raise mercenaries. Richard, however, now in league with his father, bore down ruthlessly on his father's enemies, and saved the situation by relentless activity in the field while his father continued the siege of Limoges. By the summer, Henry was beginning to gain the upper hand. Geoffrey and the young king, who had resorted to deceit from the beginning of the campaign—pretending to submit, pretending to assume the cross and to be about to go on crusade—now added sacrilege to their crimes, and plundered the rich abbey of St Martial at Limoges to pay their soldiers.

The young king, bored by being confined in Limoges, slipped out of the town and began to ravage Aquitaine. His followers—but not he himself—were excommunicated on 26 May; soon afterwards he fell sick, but as soon as he had recovered, he set off to plunder Rocamadour, where he stripped the shrine of St Amadour of its treasures and impudently replaced the sword of the great hero of epic, Roland, by his own. Soon afterwards, his sickness recurred and he halted at the little town of Martel on the north bank of the Dordogne. His condition rapidly deteriorated; he sent for his father, who, hardened by his son's earlier deceits, refused to come, but sent a bishop bearing a ring which had belonged to Henry I to show that he was the king's envoy. Early in June William Marshal came to him, and the young king made his peace with him, and on 7 June he made his confession, both in private and public. Four days later, lying on a bed of ashes as a sign of his repentance, he asked that a crusader's cloak, which he had once put on in deceit, should be put on him in earnest, charging William Marshal to fulfil his vow. A few hours later he died.

Henry, still at the siege of Limoges, was told of his son's death as he sat in a humble cottage, sheltering from the heat of the midsummer sun. A little later William Marshal came to him to describe his son's last hours: when asked to settle his debts, Henry replied: 'He has cost me enough, but I wish he had lived to cost me more.' Other people remembered only his charm and chivalry and generosity, particularly his followers, who foresaw only harsh treatment at Henry's and Richard's hands. Bertran de Born wrote an eloquent lament for him:

> Now every grief and woe and bitterness,
> The sum of tears that this sad century's shed,
> Seem light against the death of the young king,
> And prowess mourns, youth stands sorrowful;
> No man rejoices in these bitter days.

William Marshal, who knew both his virtues and faults, was to look back in his old age on the days when he and the young king had ridden to tournaments together as a kind of golden age of chivalry. The common people, too, mourned him as a hero, even as a kind of saint when reports of his last days began to circulate. There were rumors of miracles, and as the funeral cortege passed through Le Mans on its way to Rouen, where the young king had asked to be buried, the men of Le Mans seized the coffin and interred it as a holy relic in their cathedral. Henry, both out of respect for his son's wishes and not wishing to have another shrine like that of Becket in his lands, had the coffin dug up and buried at Rouen.

Henry now had the opportunity of re-establishing good relations with his heir. But Richard was not much easier to work with than the young king had been: his intransigence had, after all, brought about the war in the first place, and he and Henry were of different temperaments. Richard had been close to Eleanor, and had inherited many of her tastes, in particular a deep love for Aquitaine. He was colder and more calculating than the impetuous young king, with a determination to match that of Henry himself.

Almost at once there was a clash. Henry, holding to the plan of dividing his realms into three parts—the eldest son to have the 'ancestral lands' of England, Normandy and Anjou, and the other two to have Brittany and Aquitaine—tried to make Richard surrender his beloved Aquitaine to John, who still had no lands. Henry had thought of making John lord of Ireland, but knew that this would be a precarious and difficult existence. Richard, after asking for time to consider the idea, fled from the court to Poitou and put his castles in a state of defence. Henry continued to try to persuade Richard to give up the duchy throughout the winter; but when he sailed for England in the spring of 1184, Richard was still obstinate. Henry angrily told John to 'lead an army into Richard's land and get what he wanted from his brother by fighting for it.' There is more than a hint in Henry's remark that John had been pressing his claim to the duchy; John is said to have been Henry's favorite, and it may be that his ambitions led Henry to go against his better judgement. At all events, Henry did nothing to encourage John, who had no army of his own.

It was Geoffrey, once again, who incited trouble: and he provided John with an army from Brittany, which the two of them led into Poitou as soon as Henry was in England. Richard was more than a match for them, and at the end of the year Henry ordered all three of them to join him in England, where he announced a new plan at Christmas 1184. John was now to go to Ireland, Geoffrey was put in charge of Normandy, and Richard could go back to Poitou. But Richard and Geoffrey, who had only once briefly worked together and seem to have cordially disliked each other, remained at daggers drawn, and by April there was renewed war between them on the borders of Poitou and Brittany. Henry now decided that Richard must be separated from Aquitaine. He released Eleanor from prison, and ordered Richard to surrender the duchy 'without delay to his mother queen Eleanor, because it was her heritage; and he added that if Richard in any way delayed to fulfil this command, he was to know for certain that the queen his mother would make it her own business to ravage the land with a great host.' Richard, faced by this ultimatum, complied and made his peace.

Meanwhile, Henry was trying to unravel another matter complicated by the young king's death. Long before, the strategic castles in the Vexin had been transferred to him as the dowry of the young king's wife Margaret. Since she was now a widow, and there were no children of the match, the castles reverted to her. Henry was most reluctant to relinquish them, and at first made a payment of £2,700 per year to retain them while a more permanent solution was found. The answer, perhaps proposed by Philip Augustus, was that they should now become the dowry of his half-sister Alice, betrothed to Richard as long ago as 1161, but still, fifteen years later, not married to him. Henry accepted this, though at first he had some idea of marrying Alice to John rather than Richard.

In March 1186, however, a final version of the agreement bound Henry by oath to see that Richard and Alice were married, and implied that Richard was to have Normandy. His relations with Richard were evidently improving, for in the following month Richard was sent with a large army into Aquitaine to suppress a revolt in Quercy by the count of Toulouse. John had disgraced himself in Ireland, alienating both native chiefs (his hangers-on had mocked them for their long beards) and Norman lords, and spending his money on feasts instead of campaigning. Geoffrey, who may have hoped to inherit Normandy in the light of the events of the previous year, was discontented; Richard, by contrast, had been docile and obedient for more than a year.

Geoffrey's discontent came to a head in the summer of 1186, and he went to Paris in August, where he began to plot with Philip Augustus. The two became fast friends, and when Geoffrey was killed in a tournament Philip was inconsolable, and had to be restrained from leaping into Geoffrey's grave. With the arch troublemaker out of the way, Henry may have hoped for a more peaceful atmosphere: but the friendship of the young king and Geoffrey for Philip Augustus had left its mark on the French king.

Philip Augustus was now twenty-one, and although his relations with Henry had so far been cordial, he saw that there was great political capital to be made out of Henry's family quarrels, if only the opportunity could be found. He was ambitious and ruthless where

Louis had been easy-going and peaceable, and he was determined that the French kings should be unchallenged in their own lands. From 1186 onwards, Philip's actions clearly show that he had decided that there was no room for an Angevin empire within the realm of France: one or other must be destroyed. This resolve was not a sudden change of heart, but one that came about gradually as he disposed of the problems that beset the early years of his reign, such as the long drawn-out quarrel with the count of Flanders. By 1186, he had secured his own position and was ready to embark on greater schemes. Ironically, it was Henry who had helped him to settle the quarrel with Flanders, tirelessly acting as mediator until the differences were settled.

Whenever Angevin and French claims overlapped, Philip could hope to make political capital out of his rights as king and overlord. In addition, Henry's mysterious refusal to allow—or force—Richard to marry Alice made the Vexin a disputed area. The reasons for the failure to arrange the marriage ceremony are unknown. Gossip, and from a highly unreliable source at that, said that Henry had seduced Alice; but the French never mentioned this in their attacks on Henry. Others have suggested that Richard had taken a dislike to her; but Henry was probably playing a waiting game, knowing that Philip, always conscious of his dignity, was anxious to see his half-sister as queen of England. If so, it was a policy which in due course Philip turned adroitly against him.

The immediate point of conflict was elsewhere. Richard, with his usual enthusiasm for war, had not only quelled the count of Toulouse's revolt in the lands which the latter held in Aquitaine, but had gone on to conquer most of the count's own lands, reviving the old claims to Aquitaine's overlordship there which Henry himself had tried to enforce in 1159. Philip saw this as a threat to his own authority, and intervened as overlord of the two warring parties, ordering Richard to cease his attacks and threatening retaliation in Normandy. A period of shadow-boxing followed, until, at a conference in April 1187, Philip demanded that Richard should do homage to him for Poitou and that Alice and her dowry should be returned. Henry and Richard refused, and Philip marched into the sensitive border area of Berry, which Henry and Louis had disputed in years gone by. Henry raised an army to meet him, and an elaborate game of bluff developed as two papal legates

A knight, crusader or Hospitaller; behind him on the battlements a page holds out his helmet. Drawing by a follower of Matthew Paris, 1240. (British Library)

tried to mediate between the kings. On June 22, the two armies were drawn up in battle order outside Châteauroux, and fighting was imminent. But neither side was anxious to fight: Henry's expertise in warfare lay in sieges and skirmishes, and Philip was inexperienced. Henry asked for a truce on the grounds that he had vowed to go on Crusade; Philip granted his request, providing that he carried out his vow at which Henry withdrew it. Just as battle seemed inevitable, a truce was at last agreed, to last for two years.

In the course of the negotiations Richard and Philip had met in private for the first time in some years. They made up their differences, and Henry was much alarmed when, like the young king and Geoffrey before him, Richard disappeared to the French court with Philip, where Philip treated him with elaborate honor, 'eating from the same dish and sleeping in the same bed.' Richard, summoned by messengers from his father, did not return, but left the French court for Poitou, stopping on the way to seize the treasure kept at his father's castle at Chinon. He was putting his castles in Poitou on a war footing when a new embassy persuaded him to return to Henry and make his peace. But Philip had succeeded in sowing the seeds of doubt in Richard's mind: Henry had said nothing definite for some time about his plans for sharing out the inheritance of the Angevin empire, and Philip hinted that Henry was planning to disinherit Richard in favor of John, or at least to give John a far greater share than Richard could tolerate.

This uneasy situation was complicated by events in far-off Palestine. Henry, like most kings of the period, had always had a vague intention of going on crusade; and he also had a distant claim to the throne of Jerusalem itself after the death of his cousin Baldwin V in 1186. Indeed, in that year the patriarch of Jerusalem himself had come to offer the throne to him. The offer was rejected at a great council held in London, at which Henry put the onus of the decision on his barons: they said that it seemed better to them on both practical and religious grounds that Henry should govern his own realms well than that he should go to the East.

But in November 1187 news came of a great disaster in the east: at the battle of Hattin, Guy de Lusignan, the new king of Jerusalem, was overwhelmingly defeated by Saladin. He himself was captured, as well as the most sacred relic of the Christian world, the True Cross itself.

As soon as the news reached Richard in Poitou, he formally took the Cross and made his crusading vows. Henry appeared deeply disturbed by this impetuous action, and summoned Richard to him. He made no comment on Richard's action, except to say, after Richard had been with him for some days: 'You should have consulted me over such an important matter. But I will not stand in your way, and will do my best to help you to fulfil your vow.'

Going on crusade was a lengthy and hazardous business, and Richard was eager to depart. Henry and Philip saw matters otherwise: elaborate preparations and precautions were needed. In particular, Philip felt that the marriage between Richard and Alice must be settled before Richard left for the east. But at a conference in January 1188 arranged to discuss this, the archbishop of Tyre arrived from Palestine to plead for a crusade to be launched at once. Moved by his powerful speech, Henry and Philip now took the cross as well, agreeing to depart at Easter 1190.

Both Henry and Philip seem to have been quite serious in their vows: a crusading tax, called the 'Saladin tithe,' was raised and arrangements were put in hand for the raising and provisioning of an expedition. Richard, however, could not bear the thought of a delay of fifteen months, and begged to be allowed to go sooner. In order to do this, he asked for permission to raise money by pledging the revenues of Poitou; and he requested that his position as heir should be secured by receiving the homage of the barons of Normandy and England, just as Henry I had tried to secure Matilda's succession to the throne. His father answered curtly that they were going on crusade together, which amounted to a rejection of both requests. Richard contained his impatience and went to settle some old scores in Poitou, with the Lusignan family and with the count of Toulouse. Once again, his chastisement of the count was so enthusiastic and successful that Philip had to intervene, trying to make Henry restrain Richard: but Richard, who saw the city of Toulouse itself within his grasp, refused to listen, even though Philip was careful to offer easy terms for peace to him personally.

Philip was forced to take action by Richard's stubbornness, and struck at Berry, as he had done on the previous occasion when Richard attacked Toulouse. Richard withdrew from Toulouse to join his father, and he and Henry spent the summer in an inconclusive campaign, first in Berry, and then on the Norman border. By October both sides were weary of fighting, and Richard saw the prospect of the crusade receding yet further into the distance. A conference was held on 7 October between the two sides, and although his father opposed such a move, Richard offered to submit to Philip's judgement over Toulouse. But Philip made the mistake of thinking that he had Richard at a disadvantage and tried to press other claims, at which Richard swore at him and the proceedings broke up. However, he and Philip were soon reconciled, and Philip played on Richard's anxiety to leave for the East.

A new conference was arranged a month later, to which Richard came in Philip's company. Philip now offered to settle all differences and to leave Richard his conquests in Toulouse if Henry would recognise Richard as his heir and proceed with his marriage to Alice. The French king had found the weak spot in Henry's armor: his strategy depended on keeping Richard in suspense over his inheritance—the hungry falcon yet again!—and on delaying the marriage to retain a bargaining counter with Philip. So far, Richard had been as unwilling as his father to accept the match with Alice; but the bait was now too attractive, and he positively demanded to be given what Philip suggested, both bride and recognition. Henry could only answer that he would not consent to blackmail, though he did not reject the terms as such. Richard persisted in his demands, but Henry would say no more. Impetuously, believing that Henry really intended to disinherit him, Richard offered his sword-belt to Philip, and did formal homage to him for Normandy and Aquitaine, excluding only Henry's rights during his lifetime and the 'fealty due to his father the king.'

'Thus began the struggle which was never fought to a finish.' Richard walked away with Philip, and at the end of the year, Henry had put his domains on the defensive, expecting an attack by the pair of them. A truce was arranged until Christmas, and a meeting was to be held in early January to work out a settlement. But Henry fell ill, and the meeting was postponed at his request first until March, then until Easter. As Henry's illness dragged on, Philip and Richard regarded it as a trick to delay negotiations, and began to make raids along the border. On 4 June a meeting at last took place at La Ferté-Bernard in Maine, presided over by a legate sent by the pope, who was anxious that the quarrelling crusaders should make their peace and set out for the east. Philip offered the same terms as before, but Henry replied by offering to marry Alice to John, thus trying to separate Richard and Philip: he was in effect saying to the French king that if he abandoned Richard, terms could be arranged that would satisfy him. The papal legate, John of Anagni, threatened to put an interdict on Philip's kingdom if he did not make peace, but Philip refused to accept anything less than he demanded in the first place.

Richard and Philip had come prepared for war, and, as Henry withdrew, they attacked the castle at La Ferté-Bernard. They were already within Henry's domains, and for once, Henry was quite unprepared. His sickness was real enough, whatever Richard and Philip might claim, and he was in no mood to face them, particularly as he had only a handful of men with him. He decided to make his base at Le Mans, his birthplace, and a town of whose loyalty he was sure. The defences were hastily made ready, and Henry awaited the French attack.

It came within a few days. On 11 June, the French army appeared on the far bank of the river Huisne, which Henry had not had time to make secure. William Marshal, who was with Henry, went out to reconnoitre, and as a result of his report, Henry made a sortie, broke down the only bridge and put stakes in all the fords. That evening he gave orders that the buildings outside the city walls were to be burnt if the French attacked, so that they would not provide cover for an assault. Early the next morning, the French found an abandoned ford by the broken bridge, and were soon across the river. The suburbs were at once set on fire, but in the confusion no one noticed that the wind was changing, and the fire was carried into the city. Henry saw that there was no hope of putting out the flames, and decided to retreat northward.

Accompanied by about 700 knights, with William Marshal covering his retreat, Henry took to flight for the first time in his life. Cursing his misfortune, he turned towards the burning city, and swore that just as God had deprived him of the city he loved best in all the world, so he would deprive God of his soul. Richard rashly set out in pursuit of his father without putting on his armor. When he and his men caught up with the retreating column, Richard found himself confronted by William Marshal. Richard begged for mercy: 'By God, Marshal, do not kill me; it would not be a good deed, because I am unarmed.' 'No,' answered Marshal, 'I leave that to the devil,' and plunged his spear into Richard's horse. In the confusion that followed, Henry escaped.

At Alençon the army of Normandy was gathering. The Norman castles were secure. England was at peace. Henry was within a few miles and a few days of safety. But he turned away at the last moment, and travelling by byroads, he moved south into Anjou. It was an extraordinary decision: did he suspect treachery at Alençon? Did he hope to surprise his enemies? Or did the recurrence of his illness of the winter, which had him once more in its grip, mean that he had no will to fight and was going home to die? All three are possible, though the old deviousness is the most likely explanation. Knowing that Normandy was secure, he went where his enemies least expected him to go, hoping to bewilder them. But this time the hard riding was beyond him, and he came to the castle at Chinon to lie there for a fortnight in a fever.

Philip and Richard had succeeded in overrunning Maine, and they now moved south to the Loire. Tours fell after a brief siege, and messages were sent to Henry, demanding that he should make terms. Henry had recovered slightly, and was at Saumur when the count of Flanders and duke of Burgundy found him. He agreed to a meeting at Ballan, near Tours, the next day: but by the time he approached the meeting place, he was once more in a fever and had to rest on the way, sending messengers ahead to excuse the delay. Richard impatiently declared that it was all a feint; but as soon as Henry arrived, Philip saw that his opponent was seriously ill, and offered a cloak for him to sit on the ground. Henry refused, and his companions supported him in the saddle while terms were read to him; meanwhile, a thunderstorm rumbled in the hills of Anjou.

They were the same terms as ever, but set out with new harshness: besides the fulfillment of the marriage with Alice and Richard's recognition as heir, he was to place himself at the will of king Philip, to pay an indemnity of 20,000 marks, and to surrender key castles in pledge to Philip and Richard. Henry assented; physically, he could do no more, but his spirit was still unbroken: as he gave the formal kiss of peace to Richard, he muttered in his ear: 'God grant that I may not die until I have had my revenge on you.' His only request was that a

Clinton, one of the four vital castles on the border between Anjou and Poitou, where Henry II died. (Commissariat General du Tourisme)

list of those who were supporting Richard should be sent to him as soon as possible. Henry was too weak to ride back, and a litter was hastily found in which to take him to Chinon.

That night Henry's fever grew worse; only Geoffrey of Lincoln, his illegitimate son, and the faithful William Marshal and a few others were left to tend him. He thanked Geoffrey for his loyalty, saying that if he recovered he would make him one of the greatest men in the kingdom. A messenger arrived with the list of Richard's allies; William Marshal and the others read it, and decided to keep it from the king. But Henry insisted on its being read to him. The first name was that of John. He refused to listen to another word. The last of his sons had betrayed him, and he had no more desire to live.

He lingered, half-delirious, until the next day; in his fever, someone thought they heard him mutter 'Shame, shame on a conquered king,' while in more lucid moments he took leave of his friends and was carried to the castle chapel, where he made a brief confession and was given the Last Sacrament. He died on the morning of 6 July.

Gerald of Wales, who wrote eloquently and bitterly about Henry, says that he died while the few barons were elsewhere, and his attendants stripped the body. But he is an unreliable witness, anxious to paint a picture of fallen majesty. William Marshal's biographer says that there was some difficulty in finding suitable regalia, but apart from this mentions no untoward incidents. Henry's body almost certainly left Chinon in full royal pomp, as the cortége made its way through the narrow streets of the town, over the bridge across the Vienne and through the wooded hills south of the river to the abbey at Fontévrault where he had asked to be buried.

Chapter 4

The Crusading King

Richard, who had refused to believe that his father was seriously ill, was summoned to Fontévrault by a messenger sent by William Marshal. He arrived that night, alone. He walked straight down the church, his footsteps echoing on the stone flags, to the choir, where his father's bier lay. He stood for a moment, 'as long as it takes to say *Our Father*,' looked down at his father's face, and knelt briefly. Then he rose, and left the church as swiftly as he had come, pausing only to tell William Marshal to come with him. Gerald of Wales, who hated all Plantagenets, claimed that blood rushed from the nostrils as Richard turned away from his father's corpse, hinting at an old belief that a body would bleed in the murderer's presence. But Richard was now king, and if anyone else saw the phenomenon, they did not mention it.

Richard's first task was to secure his inheritance, and for that he needed William Marshal. He reminded William sharply of their last encounter: 'Marshal, you tried to kill me the other day; if I had not turned the lance away you would have done so. That would have been a bad day's work.' William said that if he had really wanted to kill Richard, he was skilled enough to see that his lance found its mark. Richard forgave him, and sent him as his representative to England, to secure his claim to the throne, knowing that both his friends and enemies would trust him. Richard did not pursue old quarrels; only one of Henry's followers—for what reason we do not know—was briefly imprisoned, and, most important of all, Richard was quick to make his peace with John.

Effigies of Richard I and Eleanor of Aquitaine at Fontévrault. (Archives Photographiques)

Richard now had no rivals to fear, and he was solemnly acclaimed duke of Normandy in Rouen on 20 July. On the other hand, his ally Philip was now his enemy. While Richard had been fighting Henry, Philip had supported him in order to weaken the Plantagenet power. Now Richard was as powerful as Henry had ever been, and Philip's intrigues had been in vain. So when they met at Gisors, Philip started the talks by trying to claim as his own all the land he had helped Richard conquer from Henry. Richard treated this with the scorn it deserved, and Philip did not insist. Other matters were settled satisfactorily and, feeling that his French possessions were safe for the moment, Richard crossed to England early in August.

On 1 September he entered London, where a great procession welcomed him, and on the 3rd he was crowned at Westminster with all possible ceremony. In an age when ceremony was very important, and men believed that everything had an inner meaning, being a kind of shadow of God's spiritual world, the most elaborate show and ritual was needed to convey the idea that a king was God's anointed, a ruler specially chosen by God himself. Richard's coronation was deliberately arranged to be much more impressive than those of the past, and the way in which it was organised has been the model for the coronation of the monarchs of England ever since.

First, Richard was solemnly chosen by the people as king, and acknowledged as their rightful lord. Then he swore the coronation oath: to keep the church safe and in peace, to put down all kinds of injustice, and to support everything that was just and merciful. This was followed by the crowning itself. He was anointed with holy oil and clothed in the splendid gold and crimson royal robes. He took the crown from the altar and gave it to the archbishop of Canterbury, who placed it on his head. Finally Mass was sung, while two earls held the heavy crown above the king's head.

Three days of feasting followed, and then Richard was free to start to plan the crusade which he had first taken up so impetuously two years earlier. Richard was never as concerned as Henry with the day-to-day business of ruling his great lands; he felt safe from any threat made by Philip of France, and he was now eager to be on his way to the East. Although much money had already been collected, a great deal more was needed before an army could be gathered and transported to the Holy Land. It was a long and dangerous journey both by land and sea, and there were endless provisions and equipment to be paid for. Richard used all possible methods to raise money, without thinking whether they were good or bad. Anyone who held an official position had to pay to keep his job; towns had to buy new charters confirming their privileges; men who had taken the Cross and did not want to go for one reason or another had to pay heavy fines. Richard sold royal lands, royal rights and royal privileges: 'everything was for sale—powers, lordships, earldoms, sheriffdoms, castles, towns, manors and so on.' He sold the earldom of Northumberland to the bishop of Durham, the aged Hugh de Puiset, and joked that he was clever to have made a new earl out of an old bishop. His officials were deeply worried by this: Richard was behaving as though he would never come back, because he would have no lands left from which to live if he did return. When someone pointed this out to him, Richard's only answer was: 'I would sell London itself if I could find someone to buy it.'

Emperor Frederick Barbarossa (1152-90) from a 13th century manuscript.
(Biblioteca Apostolica Vaticana)

There was great activity in France as well, because Philip had agreed to join Richard on the crusade to fulfil the vow that he too had made two years before, in very different circumstances, and with more than half an eye on the political advantages of such a move. Philip sent word to Richard that he would be ready to start out from Vézelay, in the south-east of France, on 1 April 1190. Meanwhile, the Emperor Frederick Barbarossa had set out from Germany the previous May, and at the beginning of 1190 was already at Constantinople. It seemed as though at last there was a chance that the defeat at Hattin would be avenged and Jerusalem retaken.

There were still small delays and a stream of little details to be settled; neither Richard nor Philip was ready by 1 April, and it was not until 4 July that they met at Vézelay. Richard had been given his pilgrim's staff in a ceremony at Tours two weeks before; as he leant on it, it had broken under his weight, and everyone took this as a bad omen for the journey. And though neither of the kings knew it yet, there had been a real disaster in the East. Frederick Barbarossa, who was the oldest and most respected of the Western leaders, had been drowned crossing a river in Turkey, and the huge German army was left without a proper leader. Many of the men dispersed, and only a handful went on to Tyre.

The gathering at Vézelay was vast: the tents spread out round the town itself like another, larger, multi-colored city. But once the armies began to move southwards, the problems began to appear. There were no really good roads, even in France, where the Roman roads had been numerous. Even the crossing of the river Rhône at Lyons became a challenge, because one of the arches of the little wooden bridge there gave way after the first few hundred men had gone over, leaving thousands stranded on the far side. It took three days for Richard to organise the building of a bridge of boats and to get the army on its way again.

At the end of July the crusaders reached Marseilles, then as now the chief French port on the Mediterranean. Here the bolder pilgrims took the more hazardous route and sailed direct for Acre. The boats of the time were fragile craft, helpless against the sudden storms which could blow up in the Mediterranean; and the direct voyage was frightening even to hardened sailors, who preferred to stay within sight of land.

Once the hills behind Marseilles disappeared, there was no sign of land until the coast of Palestine. But those brave enough to take this course reached Tyre only six weeks later, a welcome sight to the hard-pressed defenders of the town.

Richard and Philip had both agreed to go by the coast of Italy down to Messina in Sicily. Richard wanted to sail there direct from Marseilles, but the fleet that had set out from England had not yet arrived, and he was unable to raise enough ships to take his army. So both kings made a leisurely progress by way of Genoa along to Portofino's little hill-sheltered harbour, and down the flat coast of central Italy. At Ostia, near Rome, and again at Naples, Richard, bored by endless hours in small boats, spent a few days looking at the countryside and its sights. When he reached Salerno, just south of Naples, news at last came that his fleet had reached Messina. Richard lost no time in joining them.

Sicily was far from seeming like a foreign country to Richard. It had been conquered by Norman adventurers, rather in the way the Normans had conquered England, about a hundred and fifty years before. Richard's sister had been married to King William, who had died earlier in the year. In spite of the eastern appearance of the land, with its Greek, Italian and Arab inhabitants, its rulers were Norman barons. When Richard arrived, there was a bitter dispute over who should succeed King William, between Tancred, who was William's cousin, and Constance, who was William's aunt. Constance, in normal circumstances, should have inherited the throne, but she was married to the son of Frederick Barbarossa, and was still in Germany. Tancred had made himself master of most of the island with the support of the Greeks and Italians, who sided with him because he promised to free them from the oppression of the Norman barons. He also gained support because the Sicilians did not like the idea of becoming part of the German empire, as they would have done if Constance was their ruler.

Richard arrived in Messina in splendid style, amid a fleet of ships decorated with flags and coats of arms. The ships were mostly great galleys, rowed by bank upon bank of men pulling on huge oars. On the prow of the largest of them stood Richard himself, so that everyone could see him. It was a very different scene from Philip's landing; the French king had arrived a day or two earlier, and had slipped ashore

The Sicilian court in the 1190s, showing notaries writing in Greek, Latin and Arabic. At the bottom, King Tancred is shown receiving a copy of the manuscript; from the Chronicle of Petrus de Eboli, *c. 1200. (Bürgerbibliothek, Bern)*

unnoticed without an escort. Kings were expected to make a great display on such occasions; there was a saying which ran: 'Men are judged by their looks,' and Philip was much criticised for not looking like a king when he arrived. The difference in temperament between the two kings became more and more obvious as the expedition went on.

Richard had a reason for wanting to impress the Sicilians with his power and splendor. The king who had just died had left Henry II some valuable property in his will: a golden table twelve feet long, a silk tent that could hold two hundred men, gold dishes, and, most important of all, a number of ships fully equipped for the crusade. This the new king, Tancred, was refusing to pay; and he had taken away some of the lands which Richard's sister, Joanna, the late king's widow, should have had. To make matters worse, he had shut her up in one of his castles. So Richard had a quarrel to settle with Tancred, and with an army behind him he was determined to see that his claims were met.

Tancred did not improve matters by giving Richard lodgings outside the town of Messina, while Philip was already installed in the royal palace. So Richard lost no time in claiming the property due to him. Tancred tried to appease him by releasing Joanna and paying her a large sum of money as compensation, but this was only part of what Richard had demanded. Philip tried to calm Richard down, but without success. Richard then seized a Sicilian town in southern Italy, just across the narrow channel that separates Sicily from the mainland, and installed Joanna there with a strong garrison. Then he went back to Messina and took over a large monastery just outside the walls as his headquarters. The people in Messina now feared that he would seize the town itself, and barred the gates. Once again, Philip tried to make peace, but just as agreement seemed in sight, the townspeople started a riot outside the building where the talks were taking place. Hearing them shout abuse at the English, Richard seized his sword and ordered his men to take the town immediately. In an hour or so, it was in their hands, and much of it was in flames as the soldiers plundered houses and burnt the ships of the Sicilians. As a sign of his new conquest, Richard had his banners set on the walls.

Whatever Richard's grievances, he had gone too far. He was meant to be on crusade, not fighting another Christian king. However, it was not for this reason that Philip now quarrelled with him. The French king was angry because Richard claimed the town as his own, and had put his banners on the walls. Although Richard quickly appeased him by putting French flags there as well, one writer tells us that this was the beginning of the end of their friendship. On the other hand, Richard showed no signs of coming to terms with the Sicilians, whom he called Greeks, and built a huge wooden castle on the hills above the town, which he christened 'Mategrifon,' 'the castle that keeps the Greeks in check.' Richard loved to give such names to the castles he built, but as usual it only made the enemy more angry. It made Philip uneasy too, and he now offered Tancred his alliance against Richard. But Tancred weighed up the two kings, and decided that he would rather have Richard as an ally. So Philip's messenger was politely sent away, and Tancred made peace with Richard for another forty thousand ounces of gold, in addition to what Joanna had already been given. Tancred was not really afraid of either Philip or Richard, because he knew that they would leave Sicily soon; he was worried about the new Emperor of Germany, Henry VI, who was likely to try to claim Sicily on his wife's behalf. If Henry invaded Sicily, Tancred felt that Richard might well come to his aid, while Philip would be too cunning to get involved in such unrewarding adventures.

Philip must have been very angry when he heard of the settlement, but he said nothing. Instead, he and Richard worked together in a friendly enough fashion, organising the details of the next stage of the crusade, until Philip, for some reason or other, raised the question of Richard's marriage to his sister Alice, which was still supposed to be taking place even though it was twenty-one years since the match had been made. He may have suspected that Richard had other ideas, since Richard not only refused to think of marrying Alice, but told Philip that he was going to marry another princess, Berengaria of Navarre. Berengaria was already on her way to Sicily in the company of his mother Eleanor. There was little Philip could do, and he remained on polite terms with Richard, though he was now very distrustful of him. Both kings were anxious to be on their way again, now that winter was over. Philip was the first to leave, on 30 March. The next day, Eleanor and Berengaria arrived; they had probably waited until Philip had gone to avoid meeting him. Because it was Lent, a time when the church did not allow marriages, Berengaria accompanied Richard on his way to the East, with Joanna as her companion. Eleanor, although nearly seventy, stayed only a day or two and set off again for England, to everyone's astonishment.

The fleet that gathered in Messina harbor for Richard's departure contained over two hundred ships, a huge number for those days. There were dromonds, busses and smacks for carrying men, baggage and equipment; these were all sailing ships, slow but seaworthy. About a quarter of the fleet were warships, armed galleys propelled by rowers. Joanna and Berengaria went in a spacious dromond, the largest of the transport ships, while Richard travelled in a galley. Knowing that it would not be an easy voyage, Richard was very careful to arrange that the fleet should sail close together in squadrons. The squadrons were always to be near enough for a trumpet to be heard from one squadron to the next, and the ships in each squadron were to sail within shouting distance of each other.

At the start of the voyage, there was a calm, and the fleet had to anchor just outside Messina. Then a great storm blew up, and the ships were separated. His chaplain Ambrose wrote:

> King Richard, unmoved amid this state of confusion, continually encouraged those who were disheartened, and told them to take courage and hope that things would improve; as usual, he had a large candle in a lantern at the masthead of his ship, so that its light would direct the rest of the fleet on their way. His crew were very experienced sailors, who used all their skill to keep the ship safe in such great winds. Everyone else tried to follow the light of the king's ship, and the king ordered the crew to keep the ship stationary so that the rest could gather round, like a hen collecting her chickens.

Even so, the fleet was driven on for some days, and when Richard was able to stop and count his ships, twenty-five were missing, including the great dromond on which Joanna and Berengaria had embarked. So he decided to sail from Crete on to Rhodes and then down to Cyprus, to give the other ships a chance to catch up with him.

Richard soon had news of them, though it was not quite what he had expected. Two of the ships were wrecked near Limassol in Cyprus, and a third was saved with difficulty. This last ship was the great dromond. The men of Cyprus had taken the crews of the wrecked ships prisoner, and the other crusaders had managed to release them and barricade themselves inside Limassol harbor. But the ruler of Cyprus, Isaac Comnenus, had come down with an army and was besieging the English. Joanna and Berengaria were about to accept his offer of 'protection', which would have been captivity, when Richard arrived. He sent a message to Isaac Comnenus, saying that he was sorry to learn of the fighting between the Cypriots and his men, and asking for compensation. It was a polite message by Richard's standard, but Comnenus swore at the messenger and would not listen. Richard, furious, swiftly reacted by calling his men to arms.

It was a rash move. His men were tired after the long sea-voyage, and he had only dinghies in which to get them ashore. There was no means of landing the horses. Isaac Comnenus had a large, well-equipped army, and a barricade had been put up along the beach. Nonetheless, Richard's men fought their way through, leaping out of their little boats under cover of crossbow fire from the ships, and the Cypriot galleys were soon taken. But it was only when Richard himself waded ashore, impatient at the delay, that the Cypriots really gave way. Isaac took to flight, and despite Richard's taunts would not stay and joust with him. Richard's men gathered up a great deal of money and other valuables from the enemy camp.

Richard established himself at Limassol, and sent out a proclamation that he would fight only if attacked, and did not seek war. He was still anxious to get to Jerusalem, and the arrival of the king of Jerusalem, Guy, and other nobles from Palestine only reinforced his anxiety to be there. Philip was plotting to replace the king by another Frankish leader, Conrad of Montferrat, and Guy had come to Richard to seek his support. Before he considered his next action on the crusade, however, Richard married Berengaria in the cathedral at Limassol on 12 May. Even on crusade, Richard managed to make it a splendid ceremony: indeed, his costume was probably even more magnificent than his bride's—golden spurs, a vest of rose-colored material, studded with silver crescents, a gold-handled sword and 'a hat of scarlet, decorated with various birds and beasts in orphrey work.' She was then crowned as queen, and the next few days were passed in feasting.

Since reinforcements had arrived from Palestine, Richard now decided to capture Cyprus. The Christians in Palestine itself were holding on to a very small area of land, and were always short of supplies of food. If Cyprus was in the hands of a friendly ruler, it would be possible to send supplies across to them. So he ignored a message from Philip urging him to come to Palestine, and set out to overthrow Isaac Comnenus. He quickly took Nicosia, but there he fell ill. There were still four great castles in the north of the island to be taken, and it seemed that Isaac could defeat Richard simply by holding out, because Richard needed a rapid victory. But Guy of Jerusalem took over from Richard and captured Kyrenia castle. Among the prisoners were Isaac's wife and daughter. The Cypriots themselves disliked Isaac, who had taxed them heavily and unjustly; and Isaac soon realised that he had no hope of resisting. At the end of the month, he surrendered to Richard, who received him kindly, but insisted on putting him in chains in case he tried to escape. The only concession he would make was to give him chains of silver instead of iron, because he was a king.

Besides a great deal of wealth, Richard also secured the hoped-for food supplies by conquering Cyprus. He made sure of the island for the future, by leaving two English governors as its rulers; and he gave special instructions that regular shipments of food were to be sent to Palestine. To make sure that the inhabitants did not rebel, he promised them all their old laws and privileges. In a fortnight, Richard had won a province larger than anything else held by the Christians in the East.

He set sail again with one hundred and sixty-three ships on 6 June, and made a swift voyage until he came within sight of the coast of Lebanon the next day, with the mountains rising sheer behind. Then the fleet turned south, keeping close to the coast. As the knights sat in the shade, enjoying the cool afternoon breeze, one of the look-outs shouted that there was a foreign ship ahead. At first they took little notice; but as the ship drew closer, more and more of the knights crowded to the side to look at the strange vessel ahead: one side was green, the other yellow, and it had three great masts. It was a huge boat by the standards of the age. One of the crew hailed it, and was told that it was a French ship, belonging to the king of France. So

Richard sent over a galley; but as the crew of the galley approached, they were told that the strangers were from Genoa, on their way for Tyre. This contradiction made the crusaders suspicious; the crew of the strange ship did not look like westerners, and there was something mysterious about the boat itself. Another sailor declared: 'If they aren't Turks, you can hang me from the yardarm!' Richard ordered a small boat to row across to the strangers. As they approached, they were met with a shower of missiles, and beat a quick retreat, their suspicions confirmed.

Now the king commanded a general attack, and galleys rowed swiftly alongside. Great chains were thrown across, with hooks on the end which caught and held the other ship; and the knights and sailors swarmed up ropes and ladders in an attempt to get on board the other ship, which was much higher than the galleys. They were driven back three times, and Richard ordered the galleys to disengage and ram the ship with their great iron prows. They made great holes in her side, and soon afterwards the enemy ship rolled over and sank. Richard ordered the survivors to be taken aboard, and learnt from them that they had been sent by the brother of the Saracen commander to take men and supplies to the garrison of Acre, the town which Richard was hoping to capture. They had been waiting for a chance to enter the harbor when Richard's ships attacked them. This was a good start to the fighting, and when the crusaders landed outside Acre the next day, they were in high spirits.

The town of Acre, which the Saracens had captured from the Christians about ten years before, lay at the end of a small spit of land, partly surrounded by cliffs, with a small harbor on the side towards the land. Both the harbor and the walls on the side facing the land were surrounded by the crusaders who had already arrived. There were men of France under Philip; the Germans had replaced their lost leader, the Emperor Frederick, by various lesser princes. Their camp was on the level ground just outside the city. Beyond that, on the hills rising inland, was a more menacing sight for the newcomers: the camp of the Saracen troops under their leader Saladin.

The siege of Acre had begun two years earlier. As a result of Saladin's conquests King Guy had virtually no lands left. But he still had an army, and decided on a desperate course of action. Acre was the richest

Two Templar knights sharing a horse, from the Historia Anglorum *of Matthew Paris. The same image was engraved on the seal of the Order of Templars in memory of Hugo de Payens and Godfrey de St. Omer, the first Templars, who owned only one horse between them. (British Library)*

city on the coast, well fortified, and easily supplied from the sea, an ideal base from which to start to reconquer his lost kingdom. It was held by a strong Arab garrison, and Saladin himself was not far away with an army when Guy decided to attempt the siege. Guy was counting on help arriving from Europe in time, since the enterprise was almost impossible otherwise. Soon after he had encamped round the town, Saladin arrived and in turn besieged him, so that there were two rings of besiegers with the town in the centre. The siege had dragged on for months, with skirmishes and occasional battles, but neither side had managed to gain any advantage. Indeed, the armies were quite friendly to each other: Saracen soldiers would come to Christian feasts, and there was even a mock-combat between the children in the two camps.

Saladin, the Saracen commander, was an unusual character. He had

Crusading knights riding out of a fortified town on their way to the battle of Bocquie in Syria; from a wall-painting in the former Chapel of the Templars at Cressac in Charente, France, c. 1170-80. (Caisse Nationale des Monuments Historiques et des Sites)

risen from a humble position at the Egyptian court to become ruler of that kingdom. Although he had been ruthless in his early years, he was always gentle and courteous towards the Christians as long as they behaved in the same way to him. He disliked traitors or men who broke their word, and once killed a Christian prisoner who had betrayed his trust by executing him with his own sword. He was a devout Moslem, though his toleration of the Christians angered the really zealous warriors in his army, who were eager to fight a holy war, with no mercy shown or given. In many ways he was like Richard, though Richard lacked the religious piety which was so important to Saladin. Both were excellent generals, but Richard was hasty where Saladin was cool and calculating. Richard was more likely to win the battles, but Saladin to win the war as a whole. Richard responded to Saladin's courtesy, while Saladin respected Richard's courage and chivalry.

Richard too had his difficulties with the 'holy war' knights on his side. These were the great military orders of the Temple and the Hospital of St. John, known as the Templars and Hospitallers. In the early days of the Christian kingdom of Jerusalem, these orders had been founded to help and protect pilgrims, much as the monks in the west looked after travellers. But conditions were very different in Palestine, and pilgrims needed protection as much as food and lodging. So the monks soon employed knights to guard the travellers, and these knights became part of the monks' orders. Finally the ordinary monks almost disappeared from their ranks, and the Templars and Hospitallers became the chief fighting force of the kingdom. The only trouble with these 'crack regiments' was that they did not owe obedience to the kings of Jerusalem, but to their own Grand Masters only. It had been the advice of the Grand Master of the Temple that had led to the disaster at Hattin in 1187, the beginning of the events which had led Richard to come on crusade.

Throughout the siege of Acre, reinforcements in the shape of crusaders from the west had been arriving. As each new group arrived, they eagerly attempted to take the city and were beaten back. Only the cautious Philip had not tried this rash effort. Since he landed in April, he had spent his time reorganising the siege engines and building new towers from which to attack. He had decided to wait for Richard's appearance before launching a general assault on the town. Richard reached Acre at Whitsun 1191, and his coming put new hope into the armies. They were in a strong position, but weary from the long campaign. What they needed above all was a leader to inspire them to one last great effort.

Richard spent the first few days organising his camp, and held a friendly meeting with Philip. However, he did not improve their relationship by offering his men, and anyone else who was free to serve under him, a higher rate of pay than Philip was giving. As a result, all the unattached knights, and later even Philip's nephew, Henry of Champagne, served under Richard. A day or two later Richard's transport ships came up, bearing his siege equipment. Among the catapults, battering rams and siege towers was the wooden castle he had built in Sicily, 'Mategrifon.' This was rebuilt outside Acre. But just as all this activity was at its height, Richard had a serious illness. It was probably a kind of scurvy, caused by lack of fresh fruit on the long voyage, and by the conditions in the camp. Philip caught it too, though less seriously. Richard slowly recovered, and as soon as he was a little stronger he 'had himself carried to the front line on a silken bed …to

Defeat of the Christians and capture of the True Cross from King Guy of Jerusalem by Saladin in 1187; from Volume I of the early-13th century **Historia Maior of Matthew Paris.** *(Corpus Christi College)*

encourage his men; and from it he used his crossbow, with which he was very expert, to kill many of the enemy with its bolts.' But after this attack of scurvy, Richard's health was never very good, and he became very prone to fevers.

The old suspicion between Richard and Philip continued, although they were polite enough to each other whenever they met. Richard had sent envoys to Saladin as soon as he arrived, hoping that if he and Saladin could actually meet in person, a peaceful settlement could be arranged. Saladin cautiously replied that they ought not to meet until a truce had been fixed, and sent his brother Safadin instead. But it was just as the two kings were due to meet him that they both fell ill, and nothing came of the scheme. Philip was doubtful about Richard's dealings with the enemy, remembering how he had arranged a private peace with Tancred in Sicily in spite of him. And the old quarrel over the kingdom of Jerusalem itself remained unsettled, with Richard supporting Guy and Philip favoring his rival Conrad of Montferrat. Philip, perhaps getting his own back over Richard's offer of higher pay, ordered a general attack on the city while Richard was too ill to take part. A few days later the count of Flanders died, and there were new arguments over the inheritance of his lands.

Inside the city, however, the situation was becoming serious. With Richard's arrival, the crusaders now had enough ships to control the seas, and to prevent food supplies from reaching the defenders. On 3

The fortress of Crac des Chevaliers in Palestine, from the southwest; built c. 1200. (A.F. Kersting)

July, a great breach in the city walls was at last made by the siege machines. When the crusaders tried to force their way in, they were driven off, but it was the last straw for the defenders, who now decided to surrender. They sent to Saladin a messenger who reached the Saracen camp by swimming along the shore. But Saladin could do nothing to help them, and on 11 July the city surrendered before Saladin could persuade them to continue the fight. The terms were much more generous than Saladin would have given. But he could not stop the arrangement in time, and as the terms had been made in his name by his officers, he held to them. Acre with all its stores and military supplies was to be surrendered, 200,000 gold pieces were to be paid to the Crusaders, fifteen hundred Christian prisoners were to be released. As important as all of these, the precious relic of the True Cross, captured at Hattin, was to be returned. This fragment of the cross on which Jesus had been crucified had been the symbol of the kingdom of Jerusalem, and its capture at Hattin had caused as much dismay as the loss of the Holy City itself.

With this victory achieved, Philip was anxious to make his way home. He had been ill ever since his arrival, and he was concerned about the state of affairs in France. He said nothing to Richard, but left for Tyre with Conrad of Montferrat, and set sail from there on 3 August. The crusaders were furious but there was nothing to be done; and in some ways his departure was a good thing, particularly as Richard was left as the undisputed leader of the crusade. His only possible rival was Conrad, who was now away from the army as well.

Saladin had agreed to keep to the terms agreed for the surrender of Acre, but the arrangements did not work smoothly. The first batch of Christian prisoners were sent down from the Saracen camp on 11 August, but some of the nobles who should have been among them were not there. So Richard refused to release the captives taken at Acre until Saladin produced the missing men. Saladin replied by offering hostages instead, and the talks broke down. Ten days later Richard declared that Saladin had broken his word, and gave orders for the prisoners to be massacred. This act of cruelty contrasted sharply with Saladin's courtesy. The only excuse that Richard had was that his army was short of food. He wanted to move from Acre, and could not take the prisoners with him. The common soldiers could not understand Richard's usual tolerance: 'They marched forward with delight to fulfil his commands, and to get their own back, with God's blessing, by taking revenge on those who had killed so many Christians with their bows and crossbows.'

At long last Richard was free to set out on his march towards Jerusalem, choosing to take the road which ran down the coast, past Haifa. Beyond Haifa, he continued along the shore to Caesarea. Saladin had been following Richard's movements with the help of his scouts, and he decided that the time had come to block the crusaders' way and force a battle. On 7 September, near Arsuf, Richard realised that he could not avoid the combat any longer, and drew up his army in fighting order. It was the first major battle he had taken part in, while Saladin was a veteran commander. But Richard's long years of skirmishing and lesser warfare were good experience too. The crusading army was drawn up along the shore, and the Saracen army held the plain inland. Saladin commanded his army from a small hill nearby. The Saracens attacked first, but their foot soldiers made no impression on the Christian knights. Then Saladin sent in his Turkish horsemen, who charged the crusaders again and again. Richard would not let his men counterattack until the Turks had exhausted themselves. At last his men could stand it no longer, and moments before Richard was ready to give the order to advance, they charged. The awesome sight of the steady line of mailed horsemen, their armor gleaming in the sun, was too much for the enemy, who turned and fled. Richard hurled himself into the attack, and almost captured Saladin's camp. But Saladin managed to rally his men, and although he had to retreat, his army escaped with only a few losses.

For the crusaders, it was a great boost to their morale. Saladin was said to be impossible to defeat, and the shadow of his victory at Hattin still haunted them. Now Richard had shown them that the Saracen army could be overthrown. They went on their way in much more cheerful spirits, expecting Richard to lead them directly to Jerusalem. But he had other ideas. Though it would be quite easy to capture the Holy City, which was not very strongly defended, he knew that he would not be able to hold it if Saladin counterattacked. He would have nowhere nearby from which to obtain provisions, and Saladin could easily cut him off from his main base at Acre. So he turned aside to march on Jaffa, which he seized and started to strengthen. With this as a base, he could mount a proper attack on Jerusalem, and while Richard set himself up in Jaffa, the Saracen leader was busy strengthening the defences of the Holy City.

Richard was still hoping that an agreement might be reached with Saladin, and much of the autumn of 1191 was taken up with talks. There were times when peace seemed in sight. Richard's most surprising offer was that Palestine should be given to Saladin's brother Safadin, who would marry Richard's sister Joanna. Christians would be guaranteed access to Jerusalem, where Safadin and Joanna would live. But Joanna flatly refused to marry a Moslem, and Safadin would not become a Christian. So the talks dragged on; meanwhile the crusaders lived at ease in Jaffa, and began to forget why they had come to Palestine. There were only occasional brushes with the enemy. In one of these, Richard was nearly captured in an ambush while out hawking. Only the cunning of one of his knights, William of Préaux, saved him. William called out in Arabic that he was the 'melech' (king), and allowed the Saracens to capture him, while Richard galloped off to safety.

At the end of November, although the rainy season was just beginning, Richard at last decided to march on Jerusalem. He had

The city of Jaffa; drawing by David Roberts in 1839. (British Museum)

difficulty in gathering his army again after the months of idleness. Once they were assembled, however, the old eagerness to get to the Holy City revived. Richard was optimistic, though he was not as certain of success as his followers. News came that Saladin had disbanded some of his army and had retreated inside Jerusalem, though reinforcements were coming from Egypt to replace the men he had sent home. The moment seemed right, and Richard pressed on through stormy weather to within twelve miles of Jerusalem. He camped at the foot of the hills round the city on 3 January, and held a great council of war. He was still unsure of success: the last twelve miles were through difficult territory. Even if he pressed on and besieged the city, he might be attacked by Saladin's new troops coming up from Egypt. And if Jerusalem did fall to him, how could he hold it? His army, though full of courage, was not in good shape; many men were sick, and others had died of exposure. He was short of supplies, and did not know that Saladin was also in difficulties. For once the Templars and Hospitallers gave cautious advice. They said that Richard should go back to the coast and make sure of the cities there before he attempted to take Jerusalem. Richard asked for a plan of Jerusalem to be drawn for him,

The city of Acre; drawing by David Roberts in 1839. (British Museum)

and when he saw it he sadly admitted that he could not hope to take it with the army in its present state. So he ordered the army to retreat.

Many of the crusaders, particularly the French, were bitterly disappointed at this and withdrew from the army. Richard moved southwards with his own men and started to rebuild the fortress of Ascalon, which Saladin had dismantled a few months before. This overlooked the road from Cairo to Jerusalem, and from it Richard could hinder any army or supplies coming that way. Despite this activity, morale among the crusaders and the local nobles was low, and there were new quarrels in Acre between the supporters of King Guy and his rival Conrad of Montferrat. Conrad refused to join in the crusade, and was trying to make his own peace with Saladin. Richard was forced to go to Acre to patch up the difficulties, though he failed to obtain any help from Conrad. Realising that he would hardly be able to mount another campaign, Richard tried once again to make peace with Saladin. This time the talks went well, and a definite agreement was made. The lands Richard had conquered were to remain in Christian hands, and pilgrims would be allowed to go to Jerusalem. The Holy Cross would be returned, as previously agreed at Acre. The ambassadors took copies of the agreement away so that Saladin himself could confirm it, and everything seemed to be settled. To mark the occasion, one of Saladin's nephews was made a knight by Richard.

In the weeks that followed, Richard must have been very glad that an agreement had been reached. Messengers arrived from England, telling him that his arrangements for its government while he was away were not working. His deputy, the chief justiciar William Longchamp, had proved to be an ambitious and power hungry man, and had been deposed and imprisoned by the barons, while his brother John was now causing trouble and Richard's officers were finding it difficult to resist him. If Richard was killed on crusade, John would become king, and anyone who opposed him now would be in danger.

Richard decided that he must try to put the affairs of the Christians in the East in order, and started by trying to settle the quarrel between Conrad and Guy. Then, if he had to go home suddenly, the kingdom would at least be united and at peace. So early in April he called a great council of barons, and asked them to choose between the two men, expecting Guy to be elected. To his horror, no one wanted Guy as king, and Richard was in the embarrassing position of having to turn against the man whom he had supported ever since he arrived in Palestine. So he had to accept Conrad, and pretend that he did not mind.

But worse was to follow. At the end of the month, Conrad, who was at Tyre preparing to come down to Acre for his coronation as king, was stabbed as he walked down a narrow street in the city, and died soon afterwards. Many people thought that Richard was behind the murder, even though the men who did it belonged to the strange sect called Assassins. The Assassins were opposed to both ordinary Moslems and Christians, and held the mountainous country to the northwest of Persia. Like the Christian military orders, Templars and Hospitallers, their followers were bound to obey the master of the sect absolutely. At the time of Conrad's killing, their leader was Sheikh Sinan, whom the Crusaders called the Old Man of the Mountains. The Assassins specialised in murdering their political enemies, and never used large armies or ordinary methods of making war. Our modern word 'assassination' is a grim reminder of the success of their methods. Because they were anxious to make their sect rich, and did not regard murder as a crime, they could also be hired to kill people. Christians in the East said that this was what Richard had done, but it seems much more likely that Sheikh Sinan was settling an old quarrel with Conrad.

Conrad had been chosen king only because his wife Princess Isabella was queen in her own right. Richard soon arranged a marriage between her and Henry of Champagne, who had proved himself an able leader. He rewarded Guy with the kingdom of Cyprus, which he was finding difficult to rule. At last the problem of who should be king of the Christians in the East was solved. In the meantime, Saladin had not been in any hurry to sign the agreement drawn up in the autumn, and Richard spent the time at Ascalon, skirmishing with the enemy or hunting. As always, he was heedless of danger. One day he was nearly killed by a wild boar which he decided to hunt by himself. A little later he was ambushed early one morning as he lay asleep, but he killed four of the attackers himself; the rest were captured or fled. But this was not real warfare. If Saladin would not sign the agreement, Richard, whose men had recovered from their ordeal on the last march on Jerusalem, was eager to try to take the Holy City once again. Early in May there were rumors that a rebellion against Saladin had begun in the lands to the east of Palestine. Hoping that Saladin would be too busy dealing with the rebels to worry about the crusaders, Richard set off to take Daron. This fortress was used by the Moslems instead of Ascalon, as a place on the road from Egypt where their caravans could rest and refresh themselves after the journey through the desert. It was also Saladin's last fortress on the Palestine coast. Richard was eager to take it, so much so that he and his nobles helped the ordinary soldiers to cart the great pieces of wood which would be used to build the siege machines. The siege began on 18 May; three days later the outer wall collapsed, and on 23 May the castle was in Richard's hands.

Now the obvious target was Jerusalem. But Richard still had his doubts, and he was now worried by more bad news from England. He was ill as well; and only a fiery sermon by one of the chaplains from Aquitaine who had come with him roused him from his depression. On 7 June, the army set out for Jerusalem again, and arrived four days later at Beit-Nuba, the point at which they had turned back the last time. Here Richard once more halted. He needed time to make proper arrangements for supplies of food to be brought up to the army, and he was already short of stores. He did not know that Saladin too was in difficulty and waiting for reinforcements. The time was passed, as usual, in skirmishes, and on one of these Richard pursued a band of

Richard jousts with Saladin, from the **Luttrell Psalter.** *(British Library)*

Moslem horsemen until they were in sight of Jerusalem. Richard's companions gazed eagerly at the Holy City in the distance, but Richard himself turned away, covering his face with his shield so as not to see the city he knew he could never capture.

A few days later, however, there seemed to be a real opportunity. A great Moslem convoy had been seen by Richard's scouts making its way up the road from Egypt. Richard laid an ambush in the foothills, and after a short battle with the Egyptian troops which were escorting it, he managed to seize the whole caravan. The spoils were very rich, as much of the booty was gold and precious silks; but there were also horses and mules, which the crusaders badly needed. The reinforcements which Saladin needed were also greatly reduced. When Saladin heard the news, he seriously considered abandoning Jerusalem to the crusaders, because he did not think that he could resist them.

Richard, although delighted with his victory, was still reluctant to advance. He knew that there was no water for the army and its horses between Beit-Nuba and Jerusalem, and he was still concerned about how Jerusalem could be defended after he had gone home. There seemed no point in taking it if Saladin could recapture it without difficulty. And if the siege was more than a few days long, he would in any case have to retreat to get water and supplies. To the fury of his men, he sadly ordered the retreat on 4 July. His great expedition had failed when almost at its goal.

All that remained was to make peace with Saladin. Richard now felt free to go home; he had done his utmost to take Jerusalem, and there was nothing more he could do in the East. Saladin was also ready for peace, but he wanted the fortress at Ascalon to be demolished; if this was left intact, the Christians would control the road from Egypt to Jerusalem, and he did not want his convoys to be at their mercy. They could have the coast of Palestine, and pilgrims could come to Jerusalem as they pleased; but Ascalon must come down. Richard, knowing the value of the great fortress to the Christians, refused, and the talks broke down. Richard was now ready to leave Palestine even without an agreement, and he moved up the coast to Acre to prepare his departure.

Saladin saw this as a chance to improve his bargaining position by seizing Jaffa. In a single day's march from Jerusalem he was at Jaffa, and in three days had broken down the outer wall. The garrison agreed to surrender, but Saladin's men had got out of control, and were plundering the town. So Saladin agreed that the Christians should stay in the citadel until he could guarantee their safety. But just as the surrender was about to take place, Richard arrived. He had heard of the attack three days before, and had at once set sail to the rescue, while his main army marched down the coast. He had only 2500 men with him, and eighty knights with three horses between them. The main army had not yet arrived; but when the garrison saw Richard's ships they at once returned to the attack and nearly succeeded in driving the Moslems out of the town. Richard, who could not see the fighting, hesitated to attack the Moslems until a priest escaped from the citadel by jumping into the harbor. He landed unhurt in shallow water, and was taken to the king. As soon as Richard learnt that the garrison were still in the citadel he ordered an attack. 'God sent us here to die, if need be; shame on anyone who holds back now!' he cried, and plunged partly armed into the nearest group of Saracen soldiers, who were taken entirely by surprise. Richard's men routed Saladin's army, and prepared to defend Jaffa.

Jaffa was far from safe, however, with a huge breach in its walls. Next day, Saladin sent envoys to start the peace talks again. Richard joked about the speed with which Saladin had nearly taken Jaffa, and the speed with which he had recaptured it, 'still in his sandals', as he put it. But he agreed that peace was urgent. Once again Ascalon was the stumbling block, and nothing could be settled; Richard was relying on the arrival of his main army, which would put Saladin in a dangerous situation.

Saladin, knowing that Richard had only a handful of men, decided to attack him in the city. It was planned as a surprise assault, but a merchant saw the movement of armed men in the early morning light, and warned Richard just in time. Richard had to improvise desperately. First he planted the ground between him and the Saracens with tent-pegs which would cause the enemy horses to stumble. Then he arranged his men in two lines. The front were footsoldiers behind a line of spears driven into the ground at an angle, to break the charge of the enemy cavalry. They formed a solid wall with their shields. Behind them were the archers. The Moslems charged again and again at the line of spears and the footsoldiers, but could not break through. When they began to tire, the spearmen turned their shields aside and the archers fired volleys of arrows at the horses. Then the spearmen charged, with Richard at their head. It was too much for the weary enemy, and they turned and fled. Richard pursued them, and as they re-formed, his horse was killed under him. Saladin, who was watching, was furious with his men, who had been sullen and disobedient all day. But he could only marvel at Richard's courage. He at once sent a groom with two horses to the king, so that he could remount. The rest of Richard's men sallied out of Jaffa, and the Moslem forces retreated. The next day Saladin called off the siege and went back to Jerusalem.

Richard's victory had been won against great odds, and it was largely due to his personal skill and leadership. But it had been very demanding, and he was exhausted. Jaffa was full of unburied bodies, and the summer heat made it an unhealthy place. Richard fell seriously ill, while Saladin gathered a new army. The king was desperate for peace, but Saladin refused to yield over Ascalon. He sent Richard presents of pears and peaches as he lay on his sickbed, and even had snow brought from the nearby mountains with which Richard's drinks could be cooled. Despite this friendliness, he still would not give way in the talks, knowing that Richard would soon leave Palestine. Richard could hold out no longer, and accepted Saladin's terms on 2 September. The crusade was over.

As soon as the necessary arrangements could be made, many of

Richard's army went on pilgrimage to Jerusalem. Richard himself refused to go, reluctant to see the Holy City in Moslem hands. He declared that he would be back at the end of the peace, which was to last five years, and reconquer Jerusalem. When Saladin heard of this, he said that if he had to lose Jerusalem, he would rather lose it to Richard than anyone else. But though Saladin admired and respected Richard, he did not think that he was a good statesman. One of the pilgrims to Jerusalem was the bishop of Salisbury, who had a long talk with Saladin. Saladin repeated his admiration for Richard, but said that he thought the English king was too rash and not always very wise. If he had been talking about Richard's earlier years, this might have been fair. On crusade, Richard was much more restrained and cautious than he had ever been before. He had shown that he understood the problems of Palestine much better than most crusaders. Only in battle did he allow his 'lion heart' to gain the upper hand. Perhaps Saladin, who always commanded from the safety of his camp, was thinking of the sight of Richard at the head of his troops, in the thick of the fighting. Richard *was* rash in battles, but it was what was expected of a western leader, and it boosted his men's morale in such a way that he usually got the better of Saladin.

Once peace was made, Richard journeyed in easy stages north to Acre. Here he ransomed some captives, and paid his debts; with typical generosity, he overpaid some, so that there would be no disputes after he had gone. Joanna and Berengaria, who had been at Acre for most of the sixteen months of the crusade, sailed for home on 29 September. Richard followed on 9 October. When he arrived in Palestine, the Saracens had almost driven out the Christians; now he left behind him a kingdom which was to last for another hundred years, largely because of his accomplishments.

Chapter 5

Richard's Homecoming

*R*ichard hoped to be back in England by Christmas. He set sail direct for Marseilles, which he had almost reached when news came to him from a passing ship that there was a plot to seize him when he landed. His old enemy the count of Toulouse, probably with encouragement from Philip, was determined to take this opportunity for revenge. Richard had only a small number of men with him, and he did not dare to try to fight his way through to Aquitaine. So he turned back and went up the east coast of Italy. Why he did this is mysterious. He may have hoped to reach home by going through Germany; but he knew that he had many enemies there, and he could have sailed past Gibraltar and round the Spanish coast instead. Perhaps his sailors were frightened of the Atlantic in winter; in a small ship like theirs it could be a hazardous voyage.

As it was, Richard was shipwrecked twice in the Adriatic as he sailed up the Italian coast. Once he was driven across to Ragusa, where he vowed to found a church wherever the ship came to land. The cathedral there, built with the money he gave, stood until 1667. He was welcomed by the inhabitants of the city, which was an independent republic, and was helped on his way again. His next shipwreck was much less fortunate. The ruler of the land where he was driven ashore, count Maurice, was a relation of duke Leopold of Austria. A year and a half before, when Acre fell to the crusaders, Leopold had set his banners on the city walls beside those of the two kings, Richard and Philip. Richard, angry that a mere duke should behave as his equal,

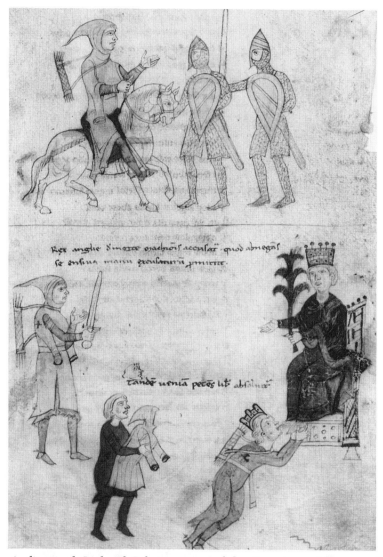

A disguised Richard I being arrested by Austrian soldiers, and making obeisance to the Austrian king Leopold in 1193; from the Chronicle of Petrus of Eboli *c. 1200. (Bürgerbibliothek, Bern)*

had hurled Leopold's banners into the ditch. Leopold left the crusade soon afterwards, swearing that he would have his revenge.

Now Richard was in the duke's lands, and he realised that he would have to disguise himself if he was to escape. He therefore sent a message to count Maurice asking for a safe-conduct for 'a merchant called Hugh and his fellow-pilgrims, returning from Jerusalem.' As was the custom, he sent a present with the message. But the ring was so precious that the count looked at it and said: 'This man is not called Hugh the merchant, but King Richard. I have vowed to seize him and his companions and to refuse their gifts, but since he has appealed to me of his own accord, he may depart.' Richard knew that this was no safe-conduct, and at once took flight, disguised as a Templar. The count followed, and managed to capture eight of the party; but Richard escaped.

Richard's road now lay through the lands of count Maurice's brother, Frederick of Pettau. The count had warned Frederick of Richard's arrival, and Frederick had ordered his men to look out for the so-called pilgrims. Soon news was brought of their arrival at the little town of Freisach. Frederick happened to have a Norman servant called Roger who had once known Richard, and he sent him to see if the king was among the newcomers, promising a huge reward if he found him. Roger recognised the king, but instead of arresting him, begged him to flee, and gave him a good horse for the purpose. He went back to Frederick and told him that the pilgrims were genuine, but Frederick did not believe him. He tried to arrest the group, but Richard and two others, one of them a boy who could speak German, got away.

The road that the fugitives found themselves on led into worse dangers still. They were approaching Vienna, the capital of Leopold himself. Although Richard and his companions tried to avoid staying in any town for long, the king was exhausted by his adventures, and decided to risk a few days' halt in a village on the outskirts of Vienna. He sent the boy into the market to change some gold coins. Unfortunately the boy was too used to being in the king's service, and behaved so proudly that the money-changer became suspicious. He managed to persuade the tradesmen that he was in the pay of a rich merchant who was on his way to the town, and he was allowed to go. He hurried back to Richard, and said that they must move on at once, but the king was still too tired to travel. On 20 December the boy went back into Vienna for the third or fourth time. He carelessly left a pair of splendid gloves belonging to Richard in his belt, and this time he was arrested by Leopold's men, who beat and tortured him until he told them where the king was. Leopold at once ordered the inn where Richard was staying to be surrounded, but when his men went in, there was only a Templar and the kitchen staff to be seen. They were puzzled for a moment, until they saw that one of the men sitting by the fire had a rich ruby on his hand: it was Richard who had disguised himself in kitchen clothes. The king managed to make them understand in broken German that he would only surrender to Leopold himself, and when the duke arrived, he gave him his sword.

Leopold at once sent Richard under close escort to the castle of Dürrenstein, ordering that the men who kept the castle should guard him with drawn swords twenty-four hours a day. The king was kept there for a fortnight, and then taken by Leopold to south Germany, where the Emperor, Henry VI, met them at Ratisbon. Henry had his own quarrel with Richard, because Richard had supported Tancred in Sicily, and Henry regarded himself as rightful king there. Henry was also in alliance with Philip, and had already written to the French king to say that 'that enemy of our Empire and disturber of your kingdom, the king of England' was in Leopold's hands. Both Leopold and Henry realised how valuable a prize Richard was. As Leopold's lord, Henry could demand that Richard be handed over to him, but Leopold wanted to extract the best possible price before he did so. It took six weeks for them to reach agreement, and meanwhile Richard went back to Dürrenstein.

Early in April, Richard was taken to the Emperor's court at Speyer, where the terms on which he would be released were read to him. They were very demanding: a hundred thousand marks of silver[*] and a large force of soldiers, the release of Leopold's cousin Isaac Comnenus of Cyprus, and a promise to help Henry conquer Sicily, as well as other conditions. On top of this, the Emperor accused Richard of betraying the crusaders by negotiating with Saladin, and of other crimes,

---

[*] A mark was eighty pence; one penny was approximately a day's wages for a laborer. The same amount of silver would be worth about £4 million today, but it is impossible to make direct comparisons of value.

King Henry VI of Germany; from a 14th century collection of lyrics in praise of love and chivalry. (Universitätsbibliothek, Heidelberg)

Dürrenstein Castle ruins, high above the river Danube in Austria.

including the murder of Conrad of Montferrat. Despite his weeks in prison, Richard replied in a magnificent speech which showed that his courage was still unbroken. Even the Emperor and his court had to applaud him. Henry could not insist on his demands, knowing that they were more than he could hope to get, and agreed to act as mediator between Philip and Richard. He gave Richard the solemn kiss of peace, and declared that if he failecd to make peace between the French and English kings, he would not take a penny of Richard's ransom. The remaining days of Easter were spent in feasting and Henry showed every sign of friendliness towards Richard. But once the holiday was over, Richard was sent off to prison once more, in the powerful fortress at Trifels nearby, perched spectacularly on a mountain top, where the imperial jewels were kept. Although escape would have been almost impossible, he was again guarded day and night, and even his own servants were kept away from him.

Meanwhile the news of the king's imprisonment had reached England, and queen Eleanor and the horrified royal officials at once tried to discover where he was being held. They sent one abbot to negotiate with the Emperor, while two other abbots searched Germany for him. A famous legend of the period tells how one of Richard's favorite minstrels, Blondel, went to find his master. He wandered through Germany, stopping outside each castle to sing a song which he and Richard had once written together. At last, when he reached Richard's prison, Richard heard him and sang the remaining verses from the window of his dungeon. This is probably no more than a good story, but Richard did write poetry while he was in prison. One piece survives, a complaint about his friends' lack of action on his behalf, addressed to his half-sister Marie de Champagne, which begins:

> *No prisoner is happy with his fate*
> *And he complains that life is misery.*
> *But to console himself, he can write songs.*
> *My friends are many, but their gifts are few:*
> *Shame on them, if for want of ransom paid,*
> *I spend two winters here.*
>
> *For all my men and barons know this well,*
> *English, Poitevin, Norman and Gascon,*
> *That I would never leave the poorest man*
> *Lying a prisoner for want of gold.*
> *Although I do not hold this against them,*
> *I am still in prison.*
>
> *Now I begin to see quite clearly that*
> *Dead men and prisoners can have no friends.*
> *Since I am here for want of coins and gold*
> *I am unhappy, and they will regret*
> *Their idleness, when I am dead and gone,*
> *In leaving me so long.*

The first messengers to reach Richard from England were the two abbots, who met him on his way to Speyer. But the king's troubles were far from over. Messengers came and went from France and England, but much of the news was bad. Philip had attacked

Normandy, and he and John had made an alliance. They were offering Henry heavy bribes to keep Richard in prison. Henry was uncertain whether he wanted Richard or Philip as an ally, but eventually decided in favor of Richard. So the captive was now moved to more comfortable quarters at Worms. On 25 June a great court was held there, and new terms were agreed for the ransom. It was fixed at a hundred and fifty thousands marks of silver, and when two-thirds of it were paid, Richard was to be set free. The emperor sent ambassadors to England to collect the money, and Richard returned to prison in the meanwhile.

Richard was now able to send messengers wherever he wanted, and he managed to do something towards restoring order in England and in his lands in France. He managed to patch up a settlement with Philip in July, which left him free to deal with John. Philip had offered him all Richard's lands in France if he would marry Alice, Richard's former fiancée, and John accepted the offer, though nothing actually came of it. Now that Philip and Richard were at peace, John decided to try and make trouble in England, hoping to prevent the ransom from being collected. He even forged the official seal of the ransom collectors and gathered the money for himself. But this was soon found out, and his attempt at rebellion was little more successful. Richard's faithful officers took most of his castles, and only two held out for any length of time, at Nottingham and Tickhill.

Meanwhile the ransom was gradually collected, though it meant a heavy burden of tax for everyone. The king had no reserves of money for huge debts like this, and his officers had to use special powers to collect a tax of one quarter of everyone's income and belongings. Only lands and houses were untaxed, and most of the tax on belongings fell on the great churches and abbeys, rich from years of gifts made by worshippers. His officials in Normandy, Anjou and Aquitaine were also busy; and as the treasure was collected it was carefully counted by the German envoys. Jewels and pieces of silver plate were all valued and noted down. By the end of the year they had gathered the hundred thousand marks needed to set the king free, and the great council at which Richard was to be released was set for 17 January.

But Philip made a desperate last bid to prevent Richard from regaining his freedom, offering a sum equal to the ransom if he was kept in prison. Henry delayed the great council until February and then announced Philip's bid in front of his barons, who were horrified by the idea of breaking the solemn agreement which they had supported. Henry resisted for two days, and finally gave in. He had one last insult for Richard, however. He suddenly demanded that Richard should do homage to him for all his lands, wherever they were, and acknowledge him as his lord. Richard, furious, took the oath; at least he knew that part of it was illegal, since he held his French lands from Philip, and that the rest of it could never be enforced. In any case, an oath forced on somebody was never regarded as valid.

So Richard at last set out on the final stage of his journey home. His mother Eleanor, still as energetic as ever, had come to meet him, and they made their way slowly down the Rhine to the coast. He used the time to make friends with the nobles of Holland, hoping to get help from them against Philip. Then after a leisurely voyage through the islands along the Dutch coast, he reached a port near Ostend where his ships were waiting. The wind was in the wrong direction, as so often happened; it was 12 March before he landed, a year and a half since he left Palestine.

On 16 March Richard made his triumphal entry into London, and a month later he held a solemn crown-wearing at Winchester. This was a ceremony which had not been held since his father's first years as king, in 1157. On such occasions the king put on his ceremonial robes to remind the people of his royal position and to impress on them that the king was subject only to God. Richard was anxious to stop any rumors that he was no longer a true king because of the homage he had done to the German emperor, and to show that he did not feel that his imprisonment had in any way weakened his claim to be an independent ruler. Richard himself loved show and splendid clothes, and it was a particularly magnificent festival, second only to his coronation.

It was also a reminder to his brother John that he was still lord of England. Richard had returned to find that John was still fomenting rebellion, and he had had to lead an army against Nottingham castle to make the garrison, who were supporters of John, give up the fortress. The other castles which John held were easier to take; the commander of one of them, Mount St Michael in Cornwall, is said to have died of fright when he heard that Richard had landed in England again.

Richard was anxious to return to France, where Philip was attacking his lands, but he had to spend another month putting affairs in England in order before he could leave. He needed to raise money, because the payment of the ransom had used up the royal treasure; this he did by selling official positions such as sheriff and imposing heavy fines on anyone who had angered him by their behavior while he was away. The sheriff was the tax-collector for a county, and had to keep order in the county, but he could make a good profit on his job because the amount he had to collect was fixed in advance. If the money he raised from a tax was greater than the fixed amount, he kept the extra money. So all the sheriffs paid to keep their jobs, because of the money they hoped to make in this way. The system was not a particularly good one, but the king had to rely on local magnates in any case, and this was at least a simple method of organising the royal revenues. As the finances of the whole country were run by a very small number of clerks in the exchequer, simplicity of operation was more important than trying to increase revenue by collecting taxes direct.

Just before his return to England, Richard had made one important appointment. The people whom he had left in charge in England had not been satisfactory: William Longchamp had been too ambitious, and the others had not been able to deal with John. So he had made the archbishop of Canterbury, Hubert Walter, the chief justiciar. Hubert was an able and energetic man, and he was now confirmed in his appointment. Ruling as the king's deputy was always a difficult job, but Hubert carried out his work so well that he remained in office for the next four years, until Richard reluctantly allowed him to resign because he was exhausted by his work.

Now Richard could turn his attention to France. On 12 May he set sail for Normandy. It was the last time he was to see England. The rest of his life was to be spent in a long duel with Philip of France, in the kind of warfare which had been his main occupation ever since his first campaigns in Aquitaine twenty-five years earlier. Philip and John had invaded Normandy again, and there were all the lands which he had lost to Philip during his imprisonment to be recaptured. Many of his barons had taken advantage of the troubles to rebel. To re-establish his father's empire would take a great deal of work, and Philip was a much more dangerous enemy than Louis VII had been.

Effigy of Archbishop Hubert Walter (d. 1205) in Canterbury Cathedral. (Conway Library)

But Richard quickly began to make good his losses. Almost as soon as he landed in Normandy, John abandoned Philip and made his peace with his brother. Philip decided to retreat when he heard this, and Richard regained much of his land. The great castle at Loches, built by his ancestor Fulk the Black, count of Anjou in the tenth century, was back in Richard's hands by the middle of June. Philip offered to talk about a truce, and soon the old pattern of fighting and attempts at making peace had set in again. It was very like the last days of Henry II a decade earlier. One week terms would be almost arranged, the next both the kings were besieging each other's castles again.

Early in July, Richard managed to catch up with Philip's army near

Vendôme, about a hundred miles south-west of Paris. He launched a surprise attack on the retreating French, and seized the carts in which the army's equipment was carried. This produced a good haul of treasure, as well as all the documents by which Philip had given lands to Norman lords who had betrayed Richard. Richard, however, was after Philip himself, vowing to capture him. A common soldier from Holland told him that Philip was a long way ahead of the army, and Richard set out in hot pursuit. He stopped only when he was deep into Philip's own lands, having tired out his horse, and left everyone else except a few companions behind. His captain, Mercadier, had to rescue him and find him another horse. Meanwhile, Philip, as cautious as ever, had taken refuge in a church near the scene of the fighting. Here he was safe from capture under the law of sanctuary. This law forbade anyone to attack a man inside a church, and was usually used by ordinary criminals: but it was hardly the behavior expected of a king.

Philip made his way safely to his own lands, and Richard turned south to Aquitaine, where an old enemy, Geoffrey of Rancogne, had stirred up trouble while he was away. With the help of Berengaria's brother, Sancho of Navarre, Richard soon took the rebel castles, including Taillebourg. This was the scene of his first triumphant siege when he was first in command of an army twenty-five years earlier. He went on to Angoulême, perched on a rocky hill high above the river Charente, which he took in a single evening. Soon most of Richard's lands were safely in his own hands again, and Philip agreed to a truce until November 1195.

The war had been brief, but expensive. Richard had exhausted most of his usual ways of raising money in the previous two years, and now had to think of special ideas for refilling his treasury. He was able to make his officers in Anjou and Aquitaine pay to keep their jobs, just as he had done with the sheriffs in England. And in England itself, he decided on a new kind of licence. Tournaments were frowned on by the church, but they were popular in France all the same. In England, the kings had always agreed with the church, and they had been illegal until now. Richard, though not as keen on them as his brother the young Henry, did not disapprove of them, and thought that they could be a good training-ground for young knights. So he now decided that anyone who wanted to hold a tournament could do so provided they bought a licence from the king, and held the tournament at one of five places named for the purpose. He also set up a commission of three leading noblemen to see that the tournaments were properly controlled, a system which worked quite well until the troubled days of Henry III's reign, when the jousts became the scene of miniature wars between rival groups of barons who were trying to seize political power.

The first six months of the next year, 1195, were among the most peaceful of Richard's life. But his health, which had been none too good even when he left on crusade, had been weakened by the fevers he had suffered at Acre and Jaffa and the hardships of the journey home and of imprisonment. He was seriously ill again in April, so badly that he almost died. People said that a hermit had warned him to mend his ways or 'God will be revenged on you.' This has been seen as a reference to Richard's reputed homosexuality. There is very little evidence for Richard's inclinations; he is known to have had an illegitimate son, even though his marriage was childless. The only actual reports of homosexuality come from biased and unreliable sources: a love of luxury and fine clothes was often associated by such writers with sodomy.

Richard certainly led a more respectable life for some time after this warning, attending church regularly and making gifts to charity. But although Richard himself was not fighting Philip, the barons on either side were still at war. Philip offered a new way of ending the long quarrel. It was based on an old kind of trial, the trial by combat. The idea was that each side chose a champion, and when these two champions fought, God would decide which side was in the right by giving their champion the victory. Philip proposed that five knights should fight on either side. Richard gladly accepted the suggestion so long as he himself could be among the five English knights and Philip among the five French knights. Philip was no great fighter, and he knew Richard's fame in the field: so the scheme was quickly dropped.

By the summer, it was clear that the truce would not last until November. Richard and Philip met at Vaudreuil on the border between their lands to discuss ways of making a permanent peace. As a first gesture of goodwill, Alice, Richard's former fiancée, who had spent all these years in English castles, was returned to her brother the French king. But there was soon trouble. The castle at Vaudreuil was technically Richard's, but Philip had recently seized it. Philip was afraid that Richard would recapture it, so he had the walls undermined while the talks went on. The castle fell down sooner than Philip had expected and Richard was furious. He declared that the truce was at an end. His men attacked Philip's army, but Philip beat them off.

All the same, the talks went on again a little later, because Richard was making secret arrangements with the German emperor to get him to attack Philip as well, and was playing for time. He managed to get the emperor to reduce by 17,000 marks the amount of his ransom that was still unpaid, on condition that he did not make peace with Philip. Nevertheless, Richard went to the next meeting with Philip as arranged. When he reached the town where they were to meet, he was met by the archbishop of Rheims who said that Philip was still taking advice from his barons and could not see him at the time arranged. This was a trick. Richard waited till the next day, and then grew impatient; but when he rode up to Philip's camp, he was told that he had broken his oath to appear on the previous day. Once again the two kings went off to raid each other's lands.

As usual, Richard had the better of the fighting. His captain, Mercadier, who commanded a force of hired soldiers from Flanders, captured the town of Issoudun on the border of the French lands and Poitou, and conquered much of Berry, a border area in central France which Richard claimed as his. Philip managed to get Issoudun back, but he reckoned without Richard, who was in Normandy. As soon as he heard of Philip's success, he left Normandy at once, and reached Issoudun, which was reckoned to be three days' ride away, in twenty-four hours. So Philip was taken entirely by surprise when he found himself confronted by Richard at the head of his men in battle order the next day. The French barons advised their king to make peace. Philip and Richard rode out alone into the field which separated their armies, and after a long conversation, they were seen by the watching soldiers to dismount, take off their helms, and exchange the kiss of peace. The terms of the peace were arranged at a meeting early in January 1196; by and large, Richard was to hold the same lands as

Henry had done, while Philip was given some disputed land on the border between his lands and Normandy.

But peace was impossible for long. Philip was determined to be lord of France, unchallenged by any rival, and to have his overlordship of Richard's lands fully recognised, while Richard was equally set on holding his own lands as an independent ruler and governing without interference from the king of France. In April, Richard tried to enforce his claim to be overlord of Brittany. His nephew, Arthur, Geoffrey's son, was only a boy, and Richard's sister-in-law ruled in his name. Richard, as overlord, had the right to arrange for the government of the duchy until Arthur was old enough to rule it himself, and he tried to enforce this. But Arthur and his supporters escaped to the French court, where Philip, who did not want to see Richard become even more powerful in France, welcomed them with open arms. Richard at once declared that Philip had broken the peace by helping his enemies.

For once, the new round of fighting did not go well for Richard. Although not such a good commander as Richard, Philip was becoming increasingly dangerous in the field. When Richard tried to come to the aid of his men besieged by Philip at Aumâle, he was driven off by the French. Soon afterwards, he was hit in the knee by a bolt from a crossbow fired by one of Philip's men, and had to spend a month in bed. Once he was better, he decided on a more permanent way of preventing Philip from attacking Normandy. Philip had gained lands which made it much easier for him to march into Normandy under the terms of the last peace; so Richard set about blocking the main way into Normandy by building a great castle above the ford near Les Andelys which was on the main route from Paris to Rouen, the capital of Normandy.

In his eagerness to start work, Richard either forgot or ignored the fact that the land on which he was building did not belong to him, but to the archbishop of Rouen. The archbishop was very angry, but Richard refused to yield. So the archbishop placed a ban on all church services in Normandy, which meant that no one could be baptised, married or buried, or receive communion; and he set out to Rome to complain to the pope. But Richard sent messengers after him, and soon made an agreement with him. Meanwhile, the king's great work continued.

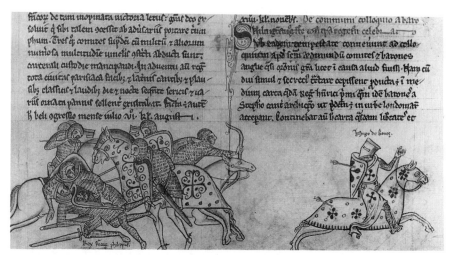

Hugh de Burgh riding away from a group of knights which includes the unhorsed King Philip of France, at the battle of Bouvines in 1214; from Volume II of the Historia Maior *of Matthew Paris, early 13th century. (Corpus Christi College)*

Richard had built castles and fortifications before, but never quite as large as this new castle. He began on the island in the middle of the Seine, called the isle of Andely. This he turned into a walled and fortified town, with an eight-sided keep to guard over it. The smaller island beside it was also fortified, forming a square of walls surrounded by the river as a moat. Above this stronghold on the river towered a huge limestone cliff commanding a great curve of river. Here Richard built the most powerful fortress of all, the 'Merry Castle' or Chateau Gaillard.

On the highest point, which jutted out from the rest of the cliff, he built a massive keep, the central part of the castle, which contained the living quarters and storerooms for the garrison. Then he dug two huge ditches in a V plan to form a triangle with the cliff face, leaving only a narrow connecting strip to the land behind. A series of outer defences ran down to the river, and even the river itself was blocked by a barrier of posts driven into the riverbed. Some of the carefully planned details may have been copied by Richard from the castles he had seen and admired in Palestine. The Christians in the East had learnt much from the Moslems; they were also much more dependent on the sheer strength of their castles. But wherever the ideas originally came from, Château Gaillard was Richard's own: when it was finished, he talked of it as 'my beautiful one-year-old daughter', and he addressed his royal letters simply 'from the fair castle on the cliff'.

Richard now turned to diplomacy as well. He was Philip's master when it came to fighting and building castles, but Philip was usually better at laying schemes and plans. What Philip won in peacetime, Richard had to take from him in war. Now the tables were turned. Richard arranged a series of alliances with the lords round the borders of Philip's lands, and he came to terms with Arthur of Brittany and his guardians. In particular he made friends with the lords of Flanders. The border between Flanders and France was difficult to defend, and Philip knew that this was a weak point. He had married Alice to the count of Ponthieu, whose lands lay at a vital point on the border. Richard promptly countered this to the south of Aquitaine, by making peace with the count of Toulouse, Raymond VIII, who had just inherited the title, and who now married Richard's sister Joanna. In return, Richard renounced his doubtful claim to be overlord of the count. Philip could no longer use his old tactic of making trouble in the south to divert Richard from raids on French lands.

As soon as spring came in 1197, fighting broke out again. Because horses had to be fed and roads were bad in winter, campaigns were almost always fought between March and October, when fodder could be found anywhere for the horses and did not have to be carted with the army, and when the roads were better. Philip nearly came to grief during this campaign. He invaded the lands of Baldwin, count of Flanders, who was now Richard's ally. Baldwin retreated towards the coast, breaking down the bridges as he went. Philip found himself trapped in the low lying part of the country in a maze of little rivers and dykes, and entirely at Baldwin's mercy. Philip had to agree to make peace to avoid being taken prisoner; the terms were to be arranged at a conference in September.

When the kings met, it was at Andely, in the shadow of Château Gaillard. Philip's men admired the castle, but Philip angrily vowed that even if the castle were made of iron he would still conquer the whole of Normandy, and Aquitaine as well. Richard, when he heard of this, swore that he would easily hold the castle against Philip, even if it were only made of butter. Both were to be proved right. Richard was to remain Philip's master in war; but Philip won Château Gaillard and most of the English lands in France after Richard's death.

Richard scored a new success in diplomacy during the truce which followed the talks. Although the German emperor had been his ally, it was never a very certain arrangement. Now Henry VI had died, and the new emperor had to be elected, since the title was not inherited but awarded by the choice of seven great princes within the Empire. After a great deal of argument, during which even Richard himself was put forward as a possible Emperor, the choice fell on Otto of Saxony, Richard's nephew, who was crowned in July 1198. Richard's sister Matilda had married Henry 'the Lion' of Saxony, a formidable man who was almost as powerful as the Emperor himself. Otto had spent most of his life at the English court, and was on excellent terms with Richard. So Richard was able to raise a new alliance against Philip, despite the fact that he was short of money and had not been able to pay his old allies the promised amount for their support.

The continual wars and intrigues were expensive, even though there were no great armies in the field. Richard had already got into trouble with the English bishops over trying to raise money for his campaigns. The bishops were great landowners, because men often gave estates to the church, and they owed the king service for these lands just like secular lords. This meant that they had to provide a number of soldiers for the king's armies. But the terms were strictly laid down, and when Richard tried to alter things to his own advantage in 1197, he was met with a firm refusal from the bishop of Lincoln, Hugh of Avalon. Hugh, who was made a saint after his death, knew that Richard would be exceedingly angry with him, and went to Normandy to put his case, quite unafraid of what might happen to him. When he arrived at the king's lodgings, he found him listening to mass, and at once demanded the kiss of peace. Richard at first refused; but at the moment in the service when the kiss was customarily given, Hugh went up to him and shook him by the cloak, until he could resist no longer and burst out laughing. The kiss was given, and after the service Hugh boldly lectured the king on his bad government. To the amazement of the courtiers, the bishop was allowed to depart unharmed, and with the assurance of the king's favor. But even though Richard gave way on this occasion, his desperate need for men and money led him to do many things which were unjust and to use every device he could think of. His only comfort was that Philip was equally hard-pressed for resources.

The summer of 1198 was peaceful, but Richard could not resist a brief campaign on the borders of France and Normandy in September. He captured two French castles, and Philip set out from Paris to drive him back. Richard went to meet him with a small band of men, and surprised him at a river crossing. He pursued him to Gisors, leading his men himself and unhorsing three French knights on the way. At Gisors there was such a scramble by the French to get into the safety of the town that the bridge collapsed under them. Richard, writing home to report his victory, said that Philip himself 'swallowed some water' and had to be dragged out by his heels, but he was not close enough to capture him. Once again Richard, in riding out with only a few men, had shown a complete disregard for his own safety, and had humiliated the enemy; but his counsellors advised him to be more careful in future. Kings were not expected to behave like ordinary knights and expose themselves to the dangers of war more than was necessary.

Towards the end of the year a truce was patched up until the following January, to be followed by a conference. The meeting was held on the Seine near Château Gaillard. Philip and Richard now distrusted each other so much that Richard remained in a boat on the river while Philip sat on horseback on the bank. Only under pressure from a messenger from the pope was the truce extended for five years, and it was clear that neither of them intended to take much notice of it. Philip was the first to break it, while Richard was in Poitou. Once again, the pope's messenger intervened and managed to arrange a permanent peace treaty, by which Philip returned all the lands he had taken from Richard in exchange for a marriage between one of Richard's nieces and Philip's son Louis. The treaty was to be sealed when Richard returned from Poitou.

In Poitou, Richard was dealing with a very minor rebellion, and was expected to return very shortly to Normandy. His opponents were two of his old enemies, but he was rumored to be more interested in a treasure which one of his barons, the lord of the little castle of Châlus, had found. Richard, always short of money, wanted to exercise his claim as overlord to a share of the treasure trove. The find, which at first was supposed to consist of a large amount of silver and gold, was later reputed to be a set of life-size golden statues of an emperor and his family. But reports about it were very vague; one version says it was discovered by a peasant while ploughing, another that the lord of the castle himself found it. There may never have been any treasure at all.

Treasure or no treasure, Richard certainly laid siege to Châlus early in March. It was one of a small group of castles south-west of Limoges all of which he attacked at the same time, so it seems that he was more concerned with putting down a rebellion than anything else. What happened on his arrival is told by the English chronicler Ralph of Coggeshall:

When Richard arrived at Châlus, he besieged one of the towers and attacked it furiously for three days, ordering his miners to undermine the tower and demolish it; which they later did. In the said tower the only soldiers or defenders were men of the viscount's guard who misguidedly helped their lord, not realising that the king was present at the siege, but thinking that it was one of his captains. While the miners were at work, the king attacked the defenders so fiercely with his crossbowmen that they scarcely dared to show themselves above the battlements or to attempt to defend the castles. All the same, the defenders occasionally terrified the besiegers by hurling huge stones down on them. After dinner on the evening of March 26, the king, unarmed except for a helmet, boldly approached the tower with his men, and attacked the besieged in the usual way with javelins and arrows. A certain soldier who had stood almost all day before dinner in one of the battlements of the tower, and had avoided harm by catching on his shield any enemy spears or arrows, watched the besiegers closely, and suddenly drew his crossbow. He fired a bolt at the king, who saw him, and cried out; the bolt struck him in the left shoulder near the vertebra of the neck, the wound curving down towards his left side, because the king had failed to stoop far enough down behind the square shield which was carried in front of him ... Later, as though nothing had happened, and while many people knew nothing of it, he entered his lodging which was nearby, and in drawing out the wooden shaft, broke it; the iron head remained in his body. So the king lay down in his chamber and a certain surgeon from the household of Mercadier operated on the king; but he made the wound much worse as he worked by the light of torches, until the injury was a fatal one. He could not easily find the iron head in the over-fat flesh, and he only got it out by using great force. Though they applied medicines and plasters diligently, the wounds began to grow worse and turn black, until they threatened to be deadly... He freely forgave the man who had fatally wounded him.

Another chronicler tells of the interview between Richard and Pierre Basile who had fired the fatal shot. When the castle was captured, Richard had him brought into his presence, and said: 'What wrong have I done you? Why have you killed me?' 'You killed my father and my two brothers with your own hand, and you would have killed me as well. Take any kind of revenge you want. You have done so much evil that now you are at death's door, I will cheerfully suffer any kind of torture.' Richard replied: 'I forgive you for killing me,' and ordered him to be set free.

This was almost his last action, for at day-close on 6 April he died, in the arms of his chaplain Miles. His mother Eleanor was with him, and it was she who accompanied his body to the great abbey church of Fontévrault in the Loire valley. Here, ten years before, Richard had stood by his father's bier; here Eleanor was now a member of the convent, having outlived her husband and all her children save John. And here Eleanor herself was to find rest before long.

Chapter 6

Lackland

*J*ohn is one of the most puzzling figures of England's history in the Middle Ages, and any account of his reign must begin by looking at the evil reputation he left behind him. Medieval men disliked violent and rapid change, and the twenty years of John's reign transformed England's politics. It was these changes, together with John's strong hand as administrator, that led him to be remembered with such hatred, and gave the gossip-mongers their opening. Henry had been unpopular in his day, but no-one could deny his greatness; Richard's charm had redeemed his lack of concern for his English subjects; but John had lost an empire, brought England under interdict, and fought with his barons. All the buried grievances of the lords against his father and brothers were vented on John, and it was their version of history, through the persuasive pages of the chronicler Matthew Paris, which prevailed.

When John came to the throne, he had already made himself a bad name. In Henry's time, when he had been sent to rule Ireland, his followers had mocked the bearded Irish chieftains who came to pay him homage. This behavior had achieved the impossible in uniting the Irish against their new Norman rulers. He left Ireland in ignominy after less than a year. Under Richard, he had openly plotted with Philip Augustus against his brother, just as Richard had plotted against Henry in their father's last years. He had shown few redeeming qualities: he had none of Richard's charm or reputation as a general, and only in

Richard's last years had he begun to throw off his fecklessness and show that there was more to him than men had thought.

When Richard died, John was thirty-two. His father had come to the throne at twenty-one, forced into maturity by circumstances. Henry had been the prospective heir since his birth; John had spent his early manhood as a possible successor to the throne, liable to be ousted at any moment if Richard had a child. This uncertainty accounts for much of John's behavior in Richard's reign: his short-term interests all too often conflicted with the long-term possibility of succession to the throne. He had never administered anything more than the kind of land-holdings that any earl would have, and even these were largely his wife's lands: hence his nickname Lackland. He had married Isabella of Gloucester, his cousin, in 1189; but the match was purely one of convenience, and as soon as he came to the throne, he used their close kinship as an excuse for divorce.

John had had a poor schooling for a future king compared with Henry's early experiences and Richard's energetic campaigns in Poitou. Despite this, John had managed to make his position as heir sufficiently secure to take over Richard's domains with very little trouble. News of Richard's death reached him as he was staying with his chief rival for the throne, his nephew Arthur of Brittany. Arthur was the son of his elder brother, Geoffrey, and the rules of feudal succession were far from clear as to whether Arthur, as the son of a man who would have inherited if he had been alive, or John, as the next of kin in the same generation, had the better claim.

John settled the matter by leaving discreetly as soon as the news arrived, and seizing the royal treasury at Chinon, just as Stephen and Henry I before him had secured the centers of government when they were faced with a disputed succession. He was helped by Richard's last command, that John should be recognised as his heir, and by the fact that during the latter part of Richard's reign he had made many friends in Richard's court. As at Henry's death, the most important figure was William Marshal, who with Hubert Walter, the archbishop of Canterbury, crossed to England to ensure John's peaceful succession. In Normandy there was no opposition; but in Anjou and Maine matters were different. Arthur's mother, Constance, with Philip Augustus' help, raised an army of Bretons, and seized Angers; as John made his way north in April, he found that Le Mans was veering towards the Breton side, and the townspeople would not admit him. Indeed, they betrayed his presence to the Bretons, and John was nearly captured. But within a week he was being acclaimed at Rouen as duke of Normandy, and was making plans to chasten the rebels in Anjou and Maine.

First, however, he had to make sure of England. A month later he had crossed the Channel and hurried to Westminster, where he was crowned on Ascension Day. Just over a fortnight later he was back in France. He was faced by a coalition as formidable as anything that Henry or Richard had had to deal with, and he was much less experienced as a soldier and politician. Philip Augustus was supporting Arthur's claim wholeheartedly, seeing an ideal opportunity for weakening the power of the Anglo-Norman empire; and it was he who posed the most serious military problem. In the long term, it was vital for John to regain Anjou and Maine from the Bretons: without them Aquitaine would be isolated from Normandy, and the defence of the southern duchy would become infinitely more difficult.

Philip opened hostilities by trying to divert John from a campaign in Maine, by attacking across the Norman border. After some indecisive fighting, a truce was arranged, but it only lasted for a few weeks, and preliminary peace talks ended with a firm rejection by John of Philip's terms, on the grounds that they were excessive. John was in a relatively strong position: he had inherited from Richard preparations for a new French campaign and a number of important allies on the eastern borders of France, who now renewed their allegiance and homage. John was thus able to ignore Philip's next attack on Normandy in September, and marched southwards. Philip was so eager to forestall him that he moved into Maine without properly co-ordinating his movements with his Breton allies. He took a castle at Ballon held by one of John's supporters, and promptly razed it to the ground instead of handing it to the Bretons. William des Roches, the Breton constable of Maine and commander of the Breton army, objected that this should not have been done without his permission; Philip gave him a short answer, whereupon des Roches made his peace with John, and negotiated a settlement between John and Arthur.

Philip had no option but to seek for peace: and in May 1200 a treaty was sealed. John had had the upper hand in the warfare, but he was

King John staghunting, from an early 14th century manuscript.
(British Library)

less successful in his diplomacy. He had hoped to be confirmed as lord
of all Richard's possessions, and to hold them on the same terms as
Richard had done, by a simple act of homage and no more. Philip,
however, brought the full weight of his status as overlord to bear, and
insisted on a much more formal relationship. John had everything to
gain from the informality of the old arrangements: homage was a
personal rather than political tie. Philip now used his position—and
he was helped in this by an increasing trend towards more specific,
written agreements—to enforce a number of definite restrictions.

John's status as vassal was underlined by an agreement that he should
pay 'relief,' a tax exacted by the lord in return for confirming a vassal
in his possessions when he inherited them. This was set at the very
substantial figure of 20,000 marks; neither Richard nor Henry had had
to pay a penny. John's relationships with his own vassals in France were
also restricted: he was not to interfere with Arthur's government of
Brittany except by agreement, and he was to pardon lords in Aquitaine

who had rebelled against him. Even his diplomatic manoevers were restricted: he agreed that his chief allies on the eastern border, the counts of Boulogne and Flanders, were rightfully vassals of the French king, and should not be encouraged by him to defy their lord.

John's acknowledgement of these conditions sprang partly from a desire for peace, and partly from the effects of Philip's consistent campaigning to make his overlordship more of a reality, which was widely approved by the French themselves. Barons in the Angevin domains had found the Angevins hard masters, always ready to suppress dissidents and to govern efficiently: they hoped that Philip's intervention would provide opportunities to play off the two kings against each other and so to regain their lost freedom. John could not hold out against his barons, who were both eager for peace and generally in favor of the new arrangements. He himself knew that Richard's extravagant adventures, his crusade and captivity, had drained the treasury and that war was a luxury he could ill afford.

The treaty was sealed on the Norman border in May 1200, and two years of peace followed. John spent these years in trying to consolidate his hold over his own vassals, with mixed results. His behavior shows a strange mixture of impulse, vindictiveness and cunning. At his best, he was an expert administrator and his father's equal as a just and able king, but this is the side of his character which is least spectacular, and therefore occupies little space in the chronicles.

Instead, we learn of his more remarkable exploits, such as his treatment of the Lusignan family. The Lusignans were the most important barons in the area round Poitiers, the capital of the duchy of Aquitaine; their powerful castle, built along a rocky ridge above the river Vonne, has vanished, but can still be seen in one of the miniatures in the *Très Riches Heures* of the Duc de Berry, painted about 1400. Their influence extended beyond their own lands, which were strategically important, because they had made a name for themselves as crusaders (we have already met Guy as king of Cyprus, and his brother Amalric was now king of Jerusalem), and Hugh's brother held the important county of Eu in Normandy. To quarrel with them was not like quarrelling with a mere local lord; but John disregarded this.

John was anxious to make peace with the count of Angoulême, the Lusignans' neighbor, and he did this by marrying the count's daughter

Isabella, even though she was engaged to Hugh de Lusignan and the only reason that she had not actually married him was her youth, for she was only twelve or thirteen. John had no such scruples; men said that he was infatuated with her from the start, and the ceremony took place within a few weeks of their first meeting, on 24 August. John probably discounted the Lusignans' reaction, seeing only the neat solution to his quarrel with Angoulême, because Isabella was the count's only child and heiress to his lands. Furthermore, until Hugh's engagement to Isabella, the Lusignans had been at daggers drawn with Angoulême, and John was only too pleased to break up this new-found and threatening alliance, particularly as Hugh would eventually have ruled both his own and Isabella's lands, lands which were as extensive as Normandy. Not content with this, John ordered his officials to harass the Lusignans whenever they could, and sought to break their power completely. Early in 1201 they appealed to Philip, accusing John of treating them unjustly. Philip was not ready to pick a quarrel with John, and at first the matter was smoothed over; Philip entertained John in lavish fashion when he visited Paris in June 1201, and both sides seemed ready to regard it as a minor incident.

John, however, was bent on the destruction of the Lusignans: he now accused them of treachery, and demanded that they fight his hired champions in a judicial duel to prove their innocence. Naturally, Hugh of Lusignan appealed to Philip again, protesting that John was misusing his powers of justice. Philip seems to have made a genuine attempt to mediate; but John, whether out of vindictiveness, stubbornness or simply a refusal to let his overlord meddle in matters which he considered to be his responsibility, would have none of it. He had misjudged the changing temper of the times: his father might have defied Louis with impunity, but Philip was a far stronger adversary, and the idea of justice as a personal right of lords was being replaced by more abstract views, which emphasized the overlord's powers. Philip now used these powers: when John failed to answer a summons to his court on 28 April 1202, the assembled barons declared John to be a rebel, and to have forfeited Aquitaine, Poitou and Anjou, since he had been summoned as lord of those lands. In the following year John was formally deprived of Normandy as well.

Philip had declared his intention of ejecting John from his French lands; the next question was whether he could carry out the sentence. At first, the usual tactics prevailed, and the Norman frontier fortresses were besieged. Arthur of Brittany, however, was for bolder moves: hoping to revive his erstwhile support in Anjou and Maine, he took a small force up the Loire and almost succeeded in capturing queen Eleanor, who had left her retreat at the abbey at Fontévrault and was heading for the safety of Poitiers. A message from her reached John near Le Mans; and in a manoever worthy of his father, he astonished the enemy by appearing from nowhere. He had in fact made a forced march of eighty miles in forty-eight hours, collecting William des Roches on the way. William agreed to help John, provided that John would accept his advice as to Arthur's fate, if Arthur were captured. Des Roches' assistance was vital, because he knew the castle of Mirebeau well. Arthur and his men had broken into the outer part of this castle, and were besieging Eleanor, who held the keep. At dawn on 1 August des Roches attacked the one gate which had not been barricaded, and in a few minutes of fighting reversed the fortunes of war: Eleanor was freed, Arthur and his supporters, including Hugh of Lusignan, were prisoners.

John had won a famous victory; but his lack of political skill showed at once. He refused to abide by his agreement with William des Roches. Des Roches may have been ambitious, and his demand for a say in Arthur's fate implies that he had something of the kingmaker in him. John, irritated by this, tried to curb him by removing Arthur from his control, and ignoring his advice in council. He had misjudgcd the temper and influence of des Roches, who rebelled in the winter of 1202-3, and persuaded the viscount of Thouars, on the border of Poitou and Brittany, to do likewise.

Once again Normandy and Aquitaine were cut off from each other, and John had no one to blame but himself. Even the defection of these leading barons would not have mattered if the lesser lords had favored John. However, from the beginning of his reign, the barons of Anjou and Maine had never favored John, for reasons which we can only guess at. They had been almost consistently loyal to Henry and Richard; they were just as consistently opposed to John. In the spring of 1203 Isabella had to be rescued from Chinon by a 'flying squad' of mercenaries, and John's supporters in the whole of the Angevin homeland held only two or three castles.

This widespread revolt disheartened John, who had never possessed his father's patience or Richard's delight in campaigning. A sustained and carefully-planned mixture of defensive and offensive action was now needed, a war of attrition and intrigue such as Henry had fought against the young king. Henry, too, had had his Mirebeau, with the capture of the king of Scots at Berwick, but he had never confused the glamour of such a victory with the hard work needed to win a war. John had no heart for such work. As Philip slowly wore away his defences, taking a castle here and advancing a few miles there, John did nothing, until the great castle of Château Gaillard was threatened. Richard had built this to be impregnable, incorporating all the latest techniques from the crusading castles in Palestine, and the only danger was that it would have to surrender for lack of supplies. John organised a bold plan for its relief: a land force would attack the French at dawn, while troops would row up the Seine, break the French barricade across the river while Philip's army was engaged, and get supplies and reinforcements into the castle. It was too bold and elaborate a scheme: the two divisions were unable to co-ordinate their attack, because the river was running too strongly and the rowers were unable to reach the castle on time. The two assaults were driven off in turn, and Norman losses were heavy.

John's next enterprise, an attack on Brittany, was equally unproductive. He now badly needed some kind of victory to re-establish his prestige. He worked industriously enough at the administration of the Norman defences, but he was unable to inspire the Norman lords to support him wholeheartedly. Just as he had lost Anjou and Maine through the barons' lack of enthusiasm coupled with his mishandling of one key figure, des Roches, so the same began to happen in Normandy: treachery was in the air. John had once again mishandled a vital figure; rumor had it that he had done far worse. Arthur of Brittany had been held captive at Rouen since the winter of 1202. Later stories said that John had ordered him to be blinded and castrated, but the castellan Hubert de Burgh had refused, and had instead put out word that Arthur was dead, in the hope of quietening the Breton revolt. By late 1203 there were certainly rumors that Arthur was dead, and these grew as time went on: Philip, in response to John's overtures for peace, would reply, 'First produce Arthur.'

Men may have believed in 1203 that John had ordered Arthur's execution, but the truth seems to have been far worse. Ten years later it was reported that John had actually killed his nephew himself, and a well-informed English chronicler, who could have got the story from William de Braose, the man who actually captured Arthur at Mirebeau, wrote that the deed had been done when John was in a drunken rage after dinner, on 3 April 1203. But one important reservation must be made about this story: de Braose, for obscure reasons, was at loggerheads with John between 1208 and 1210, when he fled to the French court, and his wife and son died in John's prisons. If the story dates from this period, de Braose is hardly a reliable witness; and it certainly seems that the French did not use the accusation of murder in their propaganda against John until after de Braose reached France. Against this, John's behavior towards de Braose is that of a man with a guilty secret, who knows that someone else is in possession of it and has determined to eliminate him. The final verdict on whether John murdered Arthur must be 'not proven.'

The effect of the rumors of Arthur's death, however, had little to do with their truth or otherwise. There is evidence that the Norman barons were growing tired of the heavy taxes and lack of freedom under the Angevin government. John was not a leader of men. Henry had awed men even when he did not inspire them. Richard had inspired them even when he did not awe them. John aroused neither inspiration nor awe. The Norman barons weighed up him and Philip, and decided that Philip looked like the winner. They were not encouraged, either, by John's treatment of the Lusignans and des Roches. Philip might be a stricter master, but he was known to be just. Once morale began to ebb, John had little hope of success. As the barons murmured, John made increasing use of mercenaries, giving them the positions of trust and responsibility the barons had once held, and increasing, in a vicious circle, the barons' resentment, as well as leaving his subjects open to the rapacity of the hired soldiers. By October 1203 such anarchy prevailed that John himself had to make detours to avoid hostile castles, and in December the king left for England: his journey to the coast

Early 13th century armor; the effigy of Robert, Lord Tattershall, at Kirkstead, Lincs. (Conway Library)

was made secretly and with undignified haste, and it was indeed a flight from the enemies who were closing in on him.

John did not return to Normandy, though he had said that he was only going to England to seek assistance. He did indeed begin preparations for a massive counterattack, to be based on Rouen and

Château Gaillard, both of which still held out. By March a considerable amount of supplies had been sent across, and John was himself preparing to cross. But it was Philip's turn to produce a military coup. Just as John's military successes were impetuous, lightning movements, so Philip's was in character, a success won by endless patience and refusal to admit that an undertaking was impossible.

On 6 March Château Gaillard, Richard's impregnable castle, was taken by storm. The French, sheltering under the bridge of rock which led to the keep, had mined their way under the walls: the defenders had driven them off by a counter-mine, but this had so weakened the foundations that Philip was able to batter down the defences of the keep by using a huge siege-engine to hurl stones at it until the wall collapsed. The garrison fought on, but were soon overwhelmed and taken prisoner. Within a month, Philip had swept in a great circle westwards to seize the heart of Normandy, and his Breton allies had joined him at Caen. The combined force swung back to Rouen, now an isolated outpost; and on 1 June the citizens of the Norman capital sent a message to say that unless John appeared before the walls within a month, they would surrender to Philip. They had so little faith in him that they handed over the keys of the town on 24 June. John's nickname of Lackland had acquired a new meaning.

John still held Aquitaine. On 1 April, Eleanor had died at Fontévrault, aged 82; active to the last, she had also lent a different kind of support to John. While she was alive, she was technically still ruler of Aquitaine, and Philip, in strict feudal law, could not seize the duchy. With her death Aquitaine too was open to his onslaught.

But here John's fortunes changed. The barons of Aquitaine weighed up the prospect of having Philip as overlord, his power reinforced by his recent victories and his center of government close at hand, and decided that they would prefer the distant king of England, separated from them by many miles of sea. John planned an expedition to counter Philip's threatened invasion of Aquitaine in the autumn of 1204, but it was not until two years later that he was actually able to leave. He reached La Rochelle on 7 June, and at once launched an attack on Montauban, on the Gironde estuary, where the king of Castile had installed a garrison as a prelude to trying to enforce a dubious claim to Gascony. The castle was reputed to be impossible to take, but it only held out against John for a fortnight. Then he made a bold foray into the heart of Anjou, holding court at Angers, before returning to his main objective, the securing of Poitou. By the end of October, most of Poitou was in his hands, and Philip agreed to a two-year truce. Well satisfied with his work, John returned to England. It was to be his last visit to the Continent for almost eight years.

Chapter 7

The King and the Barons

*J*ohn returned to England in 1204 to find the country disturbed and uneasy. The source of the disaffection was, as in Anjou and Normandy, the great barons. Many of them held estates in Normandy. They themselves had contributed to the loss of the duchy, but John was nonetheless blamed for it, even though few of them thought of it as more than a temporary confiscation. This was only one of a number of grievances, however: heavy taxation, increasing activity by government officers in spheres which the barons regarded as their own, John's personal distrust of them, all contributed to make the barons dissatisfied. John's closest friends were 'new men': William Marshal, who had begun his career as a landless knight, Geoffrey FitzPeter, who had married a lady who unexpectedly inherited the earldom of Essex, William de Braose, a minor lord from the Welsh marches.

Almost as soon as he returned, John picked a quarrel with Arthur of Brittany's stepfather, Ranulph, earl of Chester, and seized his estates. In the following March, he demanded an oath of loyalty from his chief barons; although he obtained it, he had to promise in return to 'maintain the rights of the kingdom' with their advice. News of a planned invasion, fostered by Philip, which was to be led by the heirs of king Stephen, increased John's ready suspicions. John countered rumors of invasion by a plan for a simultaneous attack on Normandy and in Poitou, and by early June a magnificent fleet had been gathered in the Solent. But the barons, although they had obeyed his summons, refused to cross the sea with him: they claimed that it was a desperate gamble when England itself was threatened, and denied that they were bound to serve him when he went abroad. Even William Marshal was reluctant to support the king's plans, because John had just quarrelled with him for trying to make peace with Philip and do homage for his Norman estates. The barons hoped for a rapid settlement, so that they could regain their lands in Normandy, and saw little prospect of John conquering the duchy. Even so, such reservations could easily have been overcome if John had enjoyed the confidence of the barons. They were adamant in their refusal, and John had to disband his troops and call off the expedition.

What is curious is that when John summoned a similar expedition in 1206, there was no resistance. We have few reliable sources for this period of John's reign, and none of them offers an explanation. The episode of 1205 may have appeared to John, with hindsight, as an isolated incident; he certainly learnt nothing from it. The success of the expedition of 1206 also made the failure of 1205 seem less important; but it was an omen of things to come.

John needed his barons' support to mount a military expedition; but he also needed their consent, or at least acquiescence, in his methods of government at home. The conflict between central government and baronial power grew steadily sharper in his reign. Inflation led to higher taxation, the search for more efficient government to royal intervention in baronial justice, which was a source of both power and income to the magnates. Inflation was an inescapable problem, but John's popularity was not enhanced by frequent 'scutages' (payments instead of service when the royal army was summoned), which were raised eleven times in seventeen years instead of twice in the decade of Richard's reign; and there were new extraordinary taxes as well, called 'gracious aids'. The money was raised efficiently and fairly; nonetheless, this was an unpleasant novelty to the taxpayers.

As to administration and justice, John took a personal interest in these, just as his father had done, an interest probably reinforced by Ranulph Glanville, who was both his tutor and the chief justiciar. Indeed, John spent far more time on the government of England than either his father or brother, and from the beginning of his reign made this his special concern. One of his first actions was to reduce the fees payable for the issue of official documents, at the suggestion of his chancellor, Hubert Walter. A charter confirming someone's right to a landholding or other property—the equivalent of title deeds today—had cost the enormous sum of £9 5s; now it was to be under £1. Also at the beginning of John's reign, copies of documents sent out by the royal officials in the chancery were kept on file. We cannot be sure that this was an innovation made by John, as earlier records may have been lost, but the earliest surviving examples of three different kinds of file all date from around 1200. The files were actually huge rolls made of pieces of parchment sewn together, like those used for keeping the royal accounts. All this points to a considerably more efficient government machine; but bureaucrats are rarely popular, and this was just as true of John's time as today.

John was doing no more than continuing his father's work, much of which had been undone during Richard's reign. Henry himself had aroused the barons' anger by his reforms, and had had to subdue the rebellion of 1173-4, despite his relatively skillful handling of his magnates. John lacked Henry's personal qualities: all accounts agree that he was unpredictable and arbitrary at times, and he led a much more luxurious existence than his father, so that it seemed as though the new taxes were being spent on feasting, jewels and clothes.

In a sense, however, John's troubles with his barons were not just a failure to manage men, but a part of a long history of simmering baronial resentment at the increasing power of the king, which went back even beyond Henry's reign to the days of his grandfather, Henry I. Now, in 1205, the barons had another grievance, the loss of their lands in Normandy; and just when John most needed his support, Hubert Walter died. Walter had fulfilled an old dream of the Angevin kings by holding office as both chancellor and archbishop of Canterbury, the dual loyalty which Becket had so carefully avoided. John was therefore anxious to find a successor who would if possible replace him in both offices, or at least continue the good relations between church and state. Unfortunately, it was no longer so easy to ensure that the royal mandate was accepted in the election of an archbishop; new rules for elections which excluded secular influence had been laid down at the Lateran Council in 1179, and the matter was complicated by the English bishops, who claimed that they should have a say in the election, which had in the past been the prerogative of the monks of Canterbury.

Even before any election could be held, the whole question of rights of election had to be referred to the pope. John was hoping to obtain the archbishopric for John Gray, bishop of Norwich; the bishops and monks, to counter this, held a secret election, and chose Reginald, prior of Canterbury, on condition that he only revealed his election if John Gray seemed likely to gain the pope's support. Reginald, however, was ambitious, and went to Rome, where he announced his election. John at once went to Canterbury and remonstrated with the monks, who denied that any election had been held. A week later they elected—in the king's presence—John Gray. But the pope, Innocent III, was a firm opponent of royal interference in elections, and quashed Gray's election. He was also suspicious of the motives behind Reginald's election, and this too was quashed. Then he asked for a new election to be held in his presence: this resulted in a tie between Gray and Reginald. So Innocent put forward a new candidate, Stephen Langton, an English cardinal well known as an author and as a teacher at the university of Paris. He was unanimously elected.

John was enraged: whatever the pope might claim as the church's right, it was at least customary to consult the king about possible candidates. He refused to confirm the election, seized the revenues of the archbishopric as though it was still vacant, and sent the monks of Canterbury into exile, to join his half-brother, Geoffrey, archbishop of York, who was likewise in royal disfavor for opposing one of John's special taxes. Both archbishoprics were therefore effectively vacant. Innocent at first tried diplomacy, hoping that John would come round to accepting Langton, whom he had recently congratulated on his appointment as cardinal. But where a matter of royal pride was concerned, John was stubborn, and by early 1208, two and a half years after Walter's death, there was no sign of agreement on the new appointment.

Innocent was not a man to sit idle in the face of such opposition. He was both a practical lawyer and an ardent advocate of reform of the church, and he had already used his ultimate weapon, an interdict, against Philip of France over the latter's bigamous marriage in 1200. It had brought Philip to heel in a matter of months. Now the same

A bell with its mouth upward and the clapper unhooked beside it, symbolizing the Papal Interdict of 1208; from the Historia Anglorum *of Matthew Paris. (British Museum)*

weapon was used against John: on 23 March 1208 the bishops of London, Ely and Worcester proclaimed an interdict. This meant the suspension of all church services: no one could be publicly baptised, married or buried in a church, no masses were said, and the only consolation for the faithful was the occasional open-air sermon in the churchyard. Baptism was performed behind locked doors, marriages at the church door, and the dead were buried in unhallowed ground, sometimes without the Last Sacrament.

But Innocent miscalculated his position. The English church had a long tradition of independence and mistrust of Rome: there was still more than a trace of the inheritance of the separate Celtic church, whose missionaries had come from Ireland to convert northern England in the sixth and seventh centuries. The sympathy of both people and clergy was by and large with the king, and the barons, who regarded the right of nominating priests to livings, or patronage, as a kind of real estate, saw the pope's interference in the Canterbury election as a threat to their own patronage.

John countered the interdict by a wholesale confiscation of church property, which could be redeemed only on payment of a fine. He even ordered that all the clergy's mistresses were to be arrested; as Innocent had been attempting, with great difficulty, to enforce the celibacy of his priests, this was a neat dig at the pope's failure to keep his own house in order. Naturally, the clergy were not slow to pay the necessary ransoms. Innocent may have been amused by this; but he was not amused by the king's successful defiance of the interdict. He had only one more weapon: excommunication of the king himself. Even Henry had been abashed by the threat of excommunication after the death of Becket, and had made his peace; but John was not to be cowed.

In this he was mistaken, because he was now open to more serious difficulties. Anyone who associated with an excommunicate was himself open to the same sentence; it was the church's equivalent of outlawry. His supporters in the English church were less enthusiastic, particularly as the interdict had lasted much longer than anyone had expected, and they were being heavily taxed as a result of it. John further alienated them by redoubling his efforts, until the demands became extortionate. If he had cause for concern over his spiritual welfare, there were no problems about his material welfare: the interdict solved his financial worries for some years.

John's relationship with his barons also grew steadily worse during these years. For reasons which are obscure, but which may have something to do with the barons' refusal to go with him to France in 1205, he began to undermine the power of William Marshal, and he pursued a vendetta against William de Braose and his family. Both Marshal and Braose held great estates in Wales, and the king's moves may have been aimed at establishing royal authority on the Welsh border. Given John's temperament, however, he may have had more personal matters in mind, seeing Marshal as ringleader of a possible barons' revolt and de Braose as a man who knew too much about his treatment of Arthur. Henry had been careful not to alienate the great barons and to punish them only for proven rebellion; John, suspicious of treachery, forestalled plots which may never have existed, and, to add insult to injury, relied on a group of ambitious, self-made soldiers who had been his mercenaries on the Continent, men such as Gerard d'Athée and Fawkes de Breauté. D'Athée undoubtedly deserved the king's good will: his spirited defence of Loches, near Tours, to the bitter end—he was taken prisoner there in 1205—contrasted with Robert FitzWalter's cowardly surrender of Vaudreuil in 1203.

John's treatment of de Braose underlies the relentlessness with which he could pursue those he distrusted. He started by demanding hostages for good behavior from him. According to a later and highly unreliable chronicle, Braose's wife refused to allow her sons to go, 'because the king basely murdered his nephew Arthur, whom he ought to have kept in honorable custody'. Whether this is true or not, John pursued Matilda with equal vehemence. When de Braose offered an enormous sum to buy himself back into the king's good will, John refused it because Matilda was still at liberty. In the spring of 1208, an expedition was mounted against de Braose, and by the autumn he and his family were forced to flee to Ireland.

The king was now involved in areas where his authority was weak. Neither Wales nor Ireland had ever been completely conquered by the Normans, and the border barons of Wales, the so-called 'marcher lords' whose lands lay along the borders ('marches'), had traditionally been allowed a degree of freedom denied to their English counterparts. In Ireland, the conquest had begun a mere forty years before, and the Angevin kings had never managed to enforce anything more than a kind of loose overlordship. John's actions in both Wales and Ireland are not dissimilar to those of Philip in France: every opportunity was taken to turn ill-defined rights of overlordship into a tangible royal presence. William Marshal, earl of Pembroke and greatest of the marcher lords, was therefore a natural target for John's manoevers; but he was too wily to be drawn into a costly conflict with the king, and discreetly spent much time on his Irish estates, while John's agents took over some of his administrative posts, such as sheriff of Gloucester and castellan of Cardigan. De Braose, on the other hand, found himself forced into open rebellion.

John suspected that a plot was being concocted between de Braose, Philip and King William of Scotland, and decided to pre-empt any action by the latter. In the summer of 1209 he raised a large army and intimidated William into handing over his two daughters as hostages for his good behavior, together with £10,000 for John's 'good will'. He then set about an expedition to Ireland, the scene of his disastrous sortie twenty-five years earlier. Henry's visit to Ireland in 1171-2 had been made in similar circumstances: John was actually excommunicate, while Henry was only threatened with such a sentence, but it is interesting that both of them, in the midst of a serious quarrel with the pope, should put themselves almost out of his reach. Henry's visit had had few lasting effects, and there was only a shadow of royal authority left, though John had appointed a new justiciar and issued new coinage.

In June 1210 he landed with a great army, and during the next few months, made royal power a reality in Ireland. He curbed the power of the English barons, and openly favored the native princes whom he had once mocked. With the latter's help, he cornered de Braose and his confederates at Carrickfergus, but de Braose himself escaped to France. His wife and son reached Scotland, but were captured and sold to John: they died of starvation in a royal prison, a story which so horrified public opinion that every chronicler of John's reign mentions the episode. De Braose's supporters, who included many of the great barons, had to buy the king's favor in the usual way; many great estates were declared forfeit and had to be paid for by heavy ransoms. The rest of the visit was taken up by measures to give Ireland an administration and legal system based on that of England, and as a parting shot a great stone keep was begun at Dublin as a tangible sign of the royal presence. Here for once John's work was genuinely creative, and the peace which prevailed in the English part of Ireland for the next century was in large measure due to him.

John now turned his attention to the independent princes of Wales, believing that he could crush them as he had crushed the Irish barons. In this he was mistaken. A first expedition into Snowdonia against Llywelyn of Powys met much the same fate as Henry's efforts there fifty years earlier: the Welsh withdrew into the mountains, leaving John's army reduced to eating their horses in order to survive. Medieval armies lived off the land, and there was nothing to plunder in the barren countryside. Nothing daunted, John launched a second expedition, better equipped for such hostile terrain, and succeeded in bringing Llywelyn to beg for terms. Llywelyn had previously been an ally of John, and the reasons for John's attack—other than those of a general ambition to complete the conquest which had eluded his father—are obscure. Terms were duly agreed, but they were punitive and not likely to lead to a lasting settlement; and in 1212 Llywelyn was to have his revenge.

By the spring of 1212 John seemed to be prospering in all he did, despite the interdict. A chronicler wrote that no one in the whole of the British Isles did not 'bow to his nod', something which none of his predecessors had ever achieved. It was time, so it appeared, to attempt to reclaim his lost lands in France, and an expedition to Poitou was put in hand. Since 1208 John had built up a considerable network of alliances, similar to the confederation of German princes organised by Richard against Philip, and this was crowned in 1211 by the defection to John's side of the count of Boulogne, once leader of a proposed invasion of England.

But just as preparations were nearly complete, news came, first of a revolt by Llywelyn, then of a plot to depose John. The army intended for France was diverted to Chester; the barons who were said to have instigated the plot against the king himself, Robert FitzWalter (the traitor at Vaudreuil in 1203) and the northern magnate Eustace de Vesci, fled into exile and their possessions were confiscated. But discontent had now spread beyond the barons: a popular preacher, Peter of Wakefield whose ascetic life and wild appearance gained him a large following, went round declaring that John would be dead before Ascension Day. At this juncture William Marshal, who had himself suffered from the king's disfavor for five years or more decided to intervene.

He organised an oath of loyalty among the barons in Ireland, and wrote to John to inform him of this, saying that he thought it was time that John made his peace with the pope. John replied warmly; and within the year, he took William's advice and sought a settlement with Innocent. There were other reasons for his change of heart: news came that Innocent was preparing to declare John formally deposed. This sentence, which would normally have carried little weight, was made more formidable by the support of Philip, who was preparing to invade England. John badly needed to secure the backing of his own barons, and it may be that he had been the first to make overtures to William Marshal, rather than the other way about. An invasion, despite John's recent successes, would have served as a focal point for baronial discontent, and many of them might have sided with the invader.

Negotiations had been going on with the pope's envoys throughout the period of the interdict. At a meeting at Northampton in August 1211, the two papal legates, Cardinal Pandulf and Durand, a member of the Order of Knights Templars, had met John and had proposed terms: John was to receive Stephen Langton as archbishop and was to reinstate the monks and other clergy who had gone into exile. He was also to compensate the church for all financial losses during the interdict. John rejected these terms as too high: they would have been a complete capitulation on his part.

Yet a year later, when Pandulf returned to England on 13 May, he accepted the terms without hesitation, such was his fear of the sentence of deposition and possible invasion. Furthermore, in a solemn ceremony at the Templar house at Ewell, near Dover, on 15 May, John became the liegeman of the Holy See for England and Ireland, by surrendering them to the pope and receiving them back in return for homage and an annual payment of 1000 marks. Later generations, tired of interference by popes who favored the French or who appointed absentee Italian prelates to English dioceses, denounced this surrender; but at the time it obtained for John the unhesitating support of Innocent. Nor was it exceptional; similar arrangements existed between the papacy and the kings of Sicily, Sweden, Denmark, Aragon and Poland. The move seems to have been made by John, at the advice of his barons, rather than suggested by Innocent: the latter's reaction was to turn from icy condemnation to a lenience and regard for the king's wishes over elections that made Langton's position—who had after all fought to keep royal interference at a minimum—very difficult in later years.

This diplomatic success was followed by a naval victory. The loss of Normandy had meant that all communications with John's remaining French lands had to be by the long sea route round Cape Finisterre, and the English navy, which had largely consisted of merchant ships commandeered for the occasion, with a handful of royal galleys, was systematically developed into a permanent force to meet this need. Instead of relying on the ships which the Cinque Ports of the south coast had to provide under the terms of their charter, John organised a system of royal galleys kept on call at ports throughout southern England, with permanent crews and commanders. Transport and passenger ships were also built. The English galleys carried out raids on French shipping in the Channel, and also acted against pirates, but the first triumph of this new force was in May 1213, when under William Longespée, earl of Salisbury, and the count of Boulogne, a fleet of 500 ships sailed for Flanders to attack the French shipping gathered for the invasion of England. The French fleet was taken by surprise in the Zwyn estuary. The small force guarding the ships was overwhelmed, and the majority of the fleet, which was said to number over 1700 ships in all, was either captured or destroyed.

The threat of invasion was removed; within two months, the excommunication on the king himself was lifted, at a ceremony performed at Winchester on 20 July by Langton. But there were still ominous rumblings of discontent from the barons. Robert FitzWalter and Eustace de Vesci had been pardoned as part of the settlement with the pope, and, perhaps through their influence, a planned expedition to Poitou was thwarted by the refusal of the magnates to accompany John, even though the fleet was in readiness at Portsmouth. John angrily set sail and went as far as Jersey before abandoning the attempt, in an even blacker mood. As soon as he returned, he set out to take revenge on the Northumbrian barons, who had been the ringleaders of the opposition, and only strenuous efforts at peacemaking by Stephen Langton led to a reconciliation.

John was still set on his expedition to Poitou, and was making active diplomatic preparations: his system of alliances in the Low Countries had come to fruition—through vast expenditure on subsidies—and during the winter a plan was made for a joint attack by the Flemish and German forces under the emperor Otto on the north-east frontier of France, and by John striking from Poitou. When John set sail in February 1214, he had every reason to be confident, even though only a handful of English barons went with him. The army was led by men whom most of the English lords distrusted and hated, such as Peter des Roches, a Poitevin who had been justiciar for only a few months. When John landed in Poitou, however, he made good the lack of support from his English lords by winning over, apparently, the majority of the lords of Poitou. A marriage was arranged between his daughter Joan and the son of his old rival Hugh of Lusignan, and John set out northwards in June, seizing Nantes, and then briefly occupying

Angers. But then disaster struck: Philip sent his son Louis with a force of 800 knights to challenge John, who was besieging a small castle outside Angers. John's army was more than adequate to meet Louis on the battlefield, but when he proposed to fight a pitched battle the lords from Poitou refused, saying that they were prepared to serve in his siege-train but not to fight in the open field. Furious at this treachery, and in serious danger, John fled to La Rochelle, where he tried to obtain reinforcements from England to continue the campaign.

While John spent his time in enforced idleness on the west coast of France, the coalition forces on the eastern frontier had moved up to invade France. Philip attacked first, however, reassured by the disappearance of the need for a rearguard action against John. He sought to prevent the coalition army from assembling, as the German forces were coming from Brussels and the English were ranged along the coast. He failed in this, and the emperor Otto and the earl of Salisbury attempted to cut off his retreat. The two armies met near Bouvines on 27 July, and in an undisciplined free-for-all lasting some three hours, both Philip and the emperor were unhorsed; but the French knights, long practised in tournaments which mimicked exactly this kind of warfare, carried the day, helped by the flight from the coalition army of the duke of Brabant. The earl of Salisbury and count of Boulogne fought on to the bitter end and were captured: Otto fled, leaving the imperial eagle standard in Philip's hands.

John's hopes, which had stood so high in February, were now dashed. His great diplomatic efforts had been wiped out, his armies were scattered; Philip was triumphant, and there was nothing for it but to accept a truce, with little prospect of mounting another expedition. The lords of the Low Countries made their peace with Philip, and Otto died four years later, overshadowed by the rising power of his rival for the imperial title, Frederick II, who was supported by both Philip and the pope. On 15 October John was back in England.

A triumph in France would probably have been an effective means of silencing the discontent among the English barons. Instead John now had to face the full tide of the barons' grievances. Matters were not improved by an attempt to raise scutage from those who had not accompanied him to Poitou; and FitzWalter and de Vesci were eager to settle old scores with John. Their demand for 'ancient liberties' and the renewal of Henry I's coronation charter was a mere smoke-screen for personal ambition. They were the spiritual heirs of the barons who had rejoiced in the anarchy of Stephen's reign, and it is noteworthy that the main support for the attack on the king came from areas where law and order had most recently been established: the north, the Welsh borders, the west country. They were condemned outright by the pope, and their attachment to the cause of liberty was chiefly a means of winning over moderate men who had little in common with their love of intrigue and violence.

What actually happened in the winter of 1214-15 is almost totally obscure. One chronicler tells how the barons pretended to go on pilgrimage to Bury St Edmunds, and there swore that if the king refused to ratify their demands in a charter, they would go to war against him. Although the writer in question, Roger Wendover, is unreliable, a draft for a charter of liberties, which has survived in the French royal archives (and whose presence there is a reminder of Philip's hand in all this) may date from this period. It contains twelve items; nine clauses apply to knights or barons only, and deal with questions of royal rights over inheritances and service. One is a general clause, against the arbitrary justice practised by the king; and two attempt to soften the severity and scope of the law in royal forests, where the preservation of the king's game took precedence over everything else. It says little about government by advice of the barons, which was to become one of the main items in the barons' programme, except that scutage rates and knight service abroad are to be regulated with their agreement—and reduced drastically from the levels demanded by John in previous years.

All we know for certain is that the barons were demanding some kind of charter of liberties in the autumn of 1214, and that discussion was put off to a formal meeting in London in January. At the January meeting, the king obtained a further delay until Easter, and the matter was referred to Innocent as the new overlord of England. De Vesci hastened to the papal court to put the barons' case, but Innocent continued to support John, and issued letters ordering the barons to desist from plotting against the king, on pain of excommunication. John ingratiated himself further with the pope by promising to go on crusade, and he took the cross on Ash Wednesday. De Vesci doubtless reported to his fellows that matters were going against them in the papal court, and by the time Innocent's letters reached England, the barons were already gathering an army at Stamford.

Beside the ringleaders of the discontented barons, many younger sons and landless knights joined their party, hoping for spoils. The king's adherents were the elder statesmen of the realm, William Marshal and his Irish friends, and seven of the great earls, who mixed uneasily with John's own friends, the 'new men' such as the justiciar Peter des Roches. John's strength lay in his castles and mercenaries; his weakness was that he could trust no man, and he could not take on the united barons of his kingdom, particularly if they had an apparently legitimate cause. He manoevred skillfully, discreetly bringing mercenaries into Ireland, where their presence would not attract attention, and delaying his reply to the barons until the pope's letters were to hand.

But the ringleaders were out for blood: at a meeting near Northampton at the end of April, they reiterated their demands. John once more rejected them, and in early May the rebels formally renounced their allegiance to him: in effect, they had declared war, and they followed this move by an attack on Northampton castle, which resisted successfully. John made no military countermove but issued letters in a conciliatory tone, offering to admit the general principle that he could only proceed against rebels or dissidents by due process of law. This was accompanied by other specific concessions, and rebels who decided to make their peace in the following weeks were treated graciously. He gave a favorable charter of privileges to London; but before most of the citizens knew about this grant, the rebels had appeared before the gates of the city, and were admitted. With the rebels entrenched in the capital, John could not hope to destroy their cause by force of arms, and conciliation would only work while he seemed to have the upper hand.

There were, however, other forces at work, men who disliked equally John's arbitrary government and the rebels' desire to bring down the lawful king by armed force. John knew that concessions had to be made, and many of the rebels were prepared to settle for such concessions. The leader of this third party was Stephen Langton, who had mediated between John and the barons before; but he had ideas of his own as to what the proposed charter should contain. The end of May and early June were taken up with discussions as to the form of the peace document, to the final form of which the king's moderate supporters such as William Marshal and the earls, and members of John's civil service, probably contributed as much as Langton or the rebels. John was not forced to sign the charter at the point of a sword, nor were the barons of England united as one against him. The document to which he set his seal on 10 June at Runnymede was a draft compromise, and an elaborate one at that, not a blunt ultimatum. Five days later the final version was ready, with minor amendments, and the barons came to meet the king for a ceremonial agreement of terms. On 19 June they renewed their oaths of allegiance to the king, and copies of the charter were distributed throughout the kingdom.

What is surprising about Magna Carta—and here the hand of Stephen Langton is most apparent—is how general its provisions are, given that it is a settlement of a dispute where details mattered more than principles. Only two or three clauses refer to specific grievances over the king's conduct and his choice of supporters: Gerard d'Athée is to be dismissed, hostages for good conduct are to be released, and mercenary forces disbanded. The charter opens, too, with a clause dear to Langton's heart, an affirmation of the liberties of the church; and only then does it go on to deal with the relationship between the king and his barons which was the nub of the quarrel. Clauses 2 to 12 and three others deal with the financial relationship between the king and lord, covering the various feudal dues and the payments of debts. Problems of administration, in the law courts, in local government and in the forest areas, occupy no less than twenty clauses: some of the grievances were minor, others substantial. The rights of cities and of merchants were touched on, and London's new charter was confirmed. All of these items are generalisations: there is no reference to specific cases.

But they are generalisations of a very narrow kind compared to the sweeping scope of the final clause, by which the charter was to be enforced. This provided that the barons were to choose twenty-five of their number, who were to be responsible for seeing that the charter was observed. Any four of these twenty-five could come to the king and point out a breach of the charter by him or his servants: and if the king failed to rectify matters within forty days, the twenty-five barons 'shall distrain and distress us in every way saving our person and the persons of our queen and our children, until, in their opinion, amends have been made; and when amends have been made, they shall obey us as before'. In one sense this was a familiar legal formula: contracts were often enforced by similar clauses of 'distraint and distress'. But it was a radical novelty when applied to the king himself. The Norman and Angevin kings had been absolute monarchs in practice; their powers were not limited by theoretical ideas, except in the eyes of the church, which set limits to all temporal and secular power. Now the king was to be placed below the law, of which he was merely the agent and guardian. That this should have happened was due not only to John's occasional dramatic acts of arbitrary government, but also to the barons' smouldering resentment of the gradual tightening of royal control which had begun with Henry's accession in 1154. Magna Carta marks the end of the Angevin vision of a strong central government controlled by the king alone.

As far as John himself was concerned, the charter was to have little effect. His agents and servants were instructed to carry out its provisions, and this they industriously tried to do. The barons elected twenty-five of their most extreme members as the guardians of law required by the charter, a clear warning that they were after the king's blood, and that the charter was by no means a final answer to their ambitions. The extremists refused to give securities for keeping the peace, as required under the charter, and some of them, who had left Runnymede before the charter was signed, repudiated the whole arrangement. They kept their private armies together, under the pretext of holding tournaments. At a council at Oxford in mid-July, they refused to give up London, which they were using as a fortified base, on the grounds that the provisions of the charter had not been carried out; and only after difficult negotiations did the moderate party persuade them to hand over the Tower of London to Stephen Langton's men. Langton and the bishops, angry at the failure of some barons to give security for peace, publicly condemned them for not having done so.

Despite John's outward acquiescence in the settlement, however, he could not resist an attempt to reassert his authority. In letters to the pope in June, he complained of the barons' behavior and of the terms they had obtained: Innocent, who had already condemned the barons,

Magna Carta, the Great Charter of King John, 1215. (British Library)

now replied by sweeping aside the charter as illegal and unjust, saying that it was extorted by force, and absolving John from his oath. He excommunicated all disturbers of the peace, and when Langton, anxious not to inflame the situation, refused to pronounce the sentences, he was suspended from his office as archbishop by the papal legate, Pandulf. At the end of the year thirty of the leaders were excommunicated by name, in addition to the general excommunication applied to them, their supporters and the citizens of London in September. Langton, the one figure who might have retrieved the situation, was on his way to Rome to appeal against his suspension.

War had broken out, after some weeks of active preparation by both sides, at the end of September. John had already suffered a serious blow when one of his most experienced mercenary captains, Hugh de Boves, was drowned off the Suffolk coast in a gale in mid-September. The barons, for their part, had also sought help abroad, openly declaring that their object was to be rid of John, and offering the English throne to Louis, Philip of France's son, who sent two contingents of mercenaries over during the winter. Encouraged by letters from Louis, they made the first move by seizing Rochester castle, in an attempt to block any attack on London by John, who was gathering his troops at Dover. John moved up promptly and besieged the new garrison, but it took him two months to starve them out, even though the barons, safely ensconced in London, made no effort to relieve the castle.

John's main support was in the south and west: the rebels controlled the north and east, de Vesci leading the northern party and FitzWalter—who liked to call himself 'marshal of the army of God'—the eastern lords. John now boldly planned a raid deep into the lands held by his opponents once he had taken Rochester, leaving William, earl of Salisbury, to keep the barons in London in check. His enemies did very little: they had no siege-train, and could not attack John's castles, while John had shown that, given time, he could take even their strongest fortresses. W. L. Warren, in his masterly biography of John, criticises him for not attempting to take London: but it would have been a formidable task, and there were few precedents for the successful capture of so large a town by siege. Furthermore, it was midwinter, when supplies were at their scarcest, and John had to feed his army. To have attempted to do this while encamped outside a well-provisioned city would have been asking for trouble: Edward III, attempting a mid-winter siege at Rheims in 1369-70, found that even the greatest army put in the field by an English king of the middle ages was no match for a well-garrisoned and supplied town.

John set off on 29 December from St Albans, and moving purposefully, he reached York early in January, laying waste the country as he went in the manner of William the Conqueror's great raid on northern England, the 'harrying of the north' in 1069-70, which had put down a similar rebellion. John also had to face a Scottish invasion; the new king Alexander had led his men as far south as Newcastle, but John swore that he would 'run the sandy little fox-cub to his earth,' and did so by mid-January, when he spent a week at the border fortress of Berwick.

John turned south again on 22 January, and, marching through Lincolnshire, was back at St Albans at the end of March. He had shown up the rebels' weakness, and had taken a number of towns, besides collecting a good deal of ransom money by allowing them to buy his good will. This revenue was particularly valuable because the rebellion had disrupted the king's normal sources of finance, and the exchequer was only partially functioning just at the time when he needed all the cash he could obtain. His next move was to make a similar show of strength in East Anglia, and he took Colchester after an eleven-day siege. The earl of Oxford came to make his peace with John, and the king seemed to be rapidly gaining the upper hand.

However, the rebels still held London, and the support promised by Louis had not yet arrived. This was to be the crucial factor in the civil war. At the end of April, Philip and his council decided to mount a full-scale invasion of England, led by Louis, on the pretext that John's murder of Arthur of Brittany meant that he had forfeited the English crown. John gathered a fleet to resist them, but a storm in the Thames estuary on 18 May dispersed and destroyed his ships, so that Louis was able to land unopposed on the Isle of Thanet. John's army still lay between the invaders and London, but, surprisingly, the king withdrew, possibly on the advice of William Marshal, who doubted the loyalty of John's mercenaries. John may have hoped that a foreign invasion would rally the country to his cause: the effect was exactly the reverse. The barons with an army behind them were far more formidable than the barons sitting in London while John ravaged the country unopposed. Men looked to their cause as the rising star, and the waverers began to desert John. His newly established influence in the south-east vanished, and many castles were handed over. Important moderate barons changed sides, including three great earls, and, as a final blow, even William, earl of Salisbury, deserted.

Yet there were still many who held out for John, even deep in the areas which the barons held: Windsor, Dover, the Cinque Ports in the south, Lincoln, Durham and Barnard castle in the east and north, all held out, and the followers of William Marshal and the earl of Chester secured the west midlands for the king. Louis had done little after his rapid progress through the south-east, and by September John had a new army in the field, with which he proposed to strike at the north and east. As the summer had progressed, events had turned in his favour once more. Quarrels between the barons and their French allies had developed. Louis had failed to take Dover, held by Hubert de Burgh for John. Some of the defectors had had second thoughts, including the earls of Salisbury and York, and two important rebel leaders, de

Vesci and Geoffrey de Mandeville, had been killed, the first attempting to take Barnard castle, the second in a tournament.

John marched first to Windsor, and raised the siege there; then he moved swiftly north to Lincoln to relieve the hard-pressed defenders led by Nicola de la Haye, who was both castellan and sheriff of Lincolnshire in her own right. From Lincolnshire, he went on 9 October to King's Lynn, where he started to organise supplies to be sent to the northern castles which still held out for him. The townsmen of King's Lynn welcomed John, and gave a great feast in his honor: John, who had been living on the rough fare of camp fires for the past few weeks, either overindulged himself or caught food poisoning, but it was not serious enough to prevent him from returning to Lincolnshire on 11 October on his way north, stopping at Wisbech to organise further shipping of supplies.

While he rode in a broad sweep south of the Wash, covering a long distance, his baggage train took a shorter route to the king's final destination for the next day, Swineshead Abbey in Lincolnshire. This entailed crossing the estuary of the river Wellstream west of King's Lynn, somewhere near Walpole St Andrew. (The precise point is difficult to determine because the shoreline of the Wash, since the draining operations of the seventeenth century, has receded much further north.) The baggage train had a long distance to cover, and low tide was not until noon; so a number of the men in charge tried to cross before the tide was fully out, only to find themselves engulfed in quicksands. The chief loss was among members of John's household, who were probably detailed to go on ahead and make arrangements for the king's arrival: and the items that travelled with him, his portable chapel with its relics and records and some household effects, were swallowed up with them. Later writers claimed that his treasure was also lost there; but unless some fortunate archaeologist finds the exact spot, we shall never know exactly what disappeared. Much of the treasure did indeed disappear between 1216 and 1220; apart from the actual crown jewels, most of this could have been melted down to pay for troops in 1216. The crown jewels, which included the coronation regalia and his grandmother's regalia as empress of Germany, might well have been among the 'relics' which the chronicler Ralph of Coggeshall says were lost.

John himself reached Swineshead safely on the night of 12 October:
it had been a long day's ride from Wisbech, his illness was growing
worse, and the news of the disaster undermined his morale. He
struggled on northwards, resting for two nights at Sleaford, and, unable
to ride, reached Newark in a litter on 16 October. Here the abbot of
Croxton, a skillful physician, was sent for; but John was already beyond
the reach of the limited resources of medieval medicine. Two days later,
having made a brief will which left the disposal of his property to his
executors, he died. In accordance with his last wishes, his body was
borne across England, under armed escort, to the cathedral at
Worcester. There he was buried in a crimson damask robe and a monk's
cowl, near the shrine of St Wulfstan, his patron saint; twenty years later
his son raised over the tomb the striking Purbeck effigy of him, whose
fierce, determined features capture something of the restless energy of
the last of the Angevin kings.

Epilogue

*J*ohn's career, with hindsight, lies under the shadow of his father's great achievements as empire-builder and lawgiver. John's chief aims were the restoration of his father's empire and the continuation of his father's work in making the crown the supreme authority within the realm in reality as well as in name. In his first objective, he was handicapped by Richard's squandering of resources on crusading; in the second, it was his own volatile character that brought him down. Henry rarely, if ever, misused his authority: the same cannot be said of John, even if chroniclers have overdone the picture of his tyranny. But beside these immediate handicaps, there were deeper currents running against John's endeavors. Henry II's empire, in an age of slow and difficult communications, was impossibly far-flung to hold together as a unit. Proximity was of enormous tactical value; and Philip Augustus in Paris could weave a spider's web of plots north, west and south, which within a radius of a hundred miles took in all the key towns of the Angevin empire. The Angevin lands were divided by the Channel, a formidable obstacle in the days of small, unwieldy ships that could barely make headway against contrary winds. And Henry's vision of kingship was contested by both church and barons: he himself had to do battle with both, but was successful where John failed.

At John's death, a prolonged civil war seemed likely: the nine-year-old king, Henry III, had apparently little chance of succeeding peacefully to the throne, and a long strife-torn minority loomed ahead. Yet within a year, the moderate barons led by the

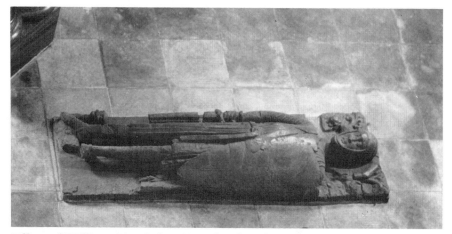

Effigy of William Marshal in Temple Church, London. (Sydney W. Newbery)

eighty-year-old William Marshal had forced Louis and his supporters to seek terms. Without the personal hatred that John had aroused—that personal hatred clearly witnessed by the stories told of him after his death, and recorded by Wendover and Matthew Paris—the royal cause flourished: Magna Carta became the royalist manifesto, and was reissued in 1217 (and again in 1220 and 1225). Men who had fought for the rebels because they seemed to offer a hope of an end to tyranny now deserted them, and after William Marshal had won a major victory at Lincoln, peace negotiations began in June 1217. They were inconclusive, and Louis raised a new mercenary army for a last effort; when this was overwhelmed at sea by an English fleet off Sandwich, he was forced to accept the terms offered, and at Kingston on Thames on 12 September, peace was made. Louis withdrew his claim, and Henry ruled unchallenged.

A complete and final compromise between king and barons was never really reached in the middle ages. Henry III's reign, however, paved the way for the union of king and lords in a common cause which marks the most prosperous moments of Edward I's and Edward III's reigns. There was to be no attempt at a return to the autocratic ways of the Angevins. The legacy of Henry and his sons to their successors was of a different kind. One part of it was the alluring, impractical claim to Henry's French domains, which was inflated to a claim to the French throne itself by Edward III. This was to be the bane of English kings for another two centuries. The other part—and far more valuable, if less exciting—was the foundation of the English systems of law and government, the work of Henry and John. Henry was the lawgiver, John the creator of an efficient administration with accurate records, so that the roots of English law are to be found in Henry's reign, but legal memory begins at the start of John's reign in 1199: anything before that date belongs to the realms of 'time immemorial'. Behind the drama of the Angevin temperament, the whims and rages and passions, lay a talent for patient, systematic, enduring work: rather than scandalous chronicles or stone effigies, this, translated into laws and methods of government, is the true monument of Henry and his sons.

Index of Main Characters

Note: members of the house of Anjou and of the English and French royal families are not included, nor are central characters described at length in the text, such as William Marshal and Thomas Becket: for these, see main index.

Alexander III Rolando Bandinelli, well known as a lawyer and diplomat, was elected pope despite the opposition of Frederick Barbarossa's ministers in 1159. Barbarossa's party elected Victor IV as pope, and the schism continued for eighteen years. Alexander's greatest achievement was the Lateran synod of 1179, at which many reforms were introduced. His diplomatic training and rational approach enabled him to steer his way through the quarrel between Becket and Henry without forcing either side to extremes; he moderated Becket's excesses and avoided a change of allegiance by Henry to Victor IV's side. He died in 1181.

Angoulême, Adhémar or Aymar, count of Adhémar rebelled against Richard and later against John in 1199; by the Treaty of Le Goulet in 1200, Philip required John to receive him back into favor, in return for refusing Adhémar's claim to hold his lands directly from the king of France. John married Isabella, his daughter, betrothed to Hugh of Lusignan; in so doing he secured Angoulême's loyalty but insulted the family of Lusignan.

Baldwin, archbishop of Canterbury Baldwin came from a poor family, and was originally a monk. He became abbot of Ford, and then bishop of Worcester, before being elected to the archbishopric in

1184. He preached the crusade with great eloquence in England after taking the cross himself in February 1188; and he accompanied Richard to the Holy Land. He was, however, shocked by the behavior of the army and of the nobles in Palestine. The strain of the journey—he was very old then—told on his health and he died in November 1190 at Acre.

Berlai, Gerald Lord of Montreuil-Bellay in the Loire valley in the 1150s, who rebelled against Geoffrey of Anjou in 1149, and held out for three years before being captured. Geoffrey refused to release him, and this led to war with Louis VII of France in 1151, ended by a peace treaty.

Bernard, St, abbot of Clairvaux St Bernard was one of the great reformers of the twelfth century. At the age of 25 he was appointed abbot of the new monastery of Clairvaux, which belonged to the recently founded Cistercian order. Under him, Clairvaux became the most important Cistercian house; he was famous for his preaching and saintly life, and this fame led to his involvement in politics, both within the church and in secular affairs. His preaching led Louis VII to take the cross in 1146 and it was partly at his urging that Louis divorced Eleanor in 1152. He died in 1153.

Blondel de Nesle A northern French poet or *trouvère*, said in a mid-thirteenth-century work to have found out Richard's whereabouts after he was captured by the duke of Austria. This he did by singing beneath the windows of each castle that he passed a song, of which only Richard knew the refrain. When he reached Dürrenstein, a voice from the castle sang the refrain, and he knew that he had found the king.

Born, Bertran de A lord and troubadour from Hautefort near Limoges, famous for his political poems or *sirventes*, which tell us much about Richard's activities in Poitou, and include a lament for the death of the young king, as well as poems reflecting the delight of the Poitevin lords in warfare.

Braose, William de Lord of lands on the Welsh border (the Marches) which he inherited in 1180, de Braose had a considerable reputation as a fighter. He was with Richard at Châlus in 1199, and enjoyed John's confidence. He captured Arthur at Mirebeau in 1202, and is believed to have given the only reliable account of the latter's fate that has survived to the monks at Margam in about 1208-10. He was given many additional lands in South Wales before his downfall in 1207.

Burgh, Hubert de Chamberlain of King John, said to have been custodian of Arthur of Brittany at Falaise, and to have refused to blind and castrate him when ordered to do so by John. He became justiciar in 1215, just after Runnymede, and early in Henry III's reign played an important part in securing peace, including winning a naval victory over the French off Sandwich in 1217.

Burgundy, Hugh III, duke of Cousin of Philip of France, who played a leading part in the Third Crusade. When Philip left after the fall of Acre, Hugh remained behind with Richard, but only reluctantly took part in the first march on Jerusalem; on the second approach to Jerusalem, it was the French who were enthusiastic to press on, and had to be deterred by Richard. He stayed in Palestine until Richard had left.

Clifford, Rosamond Mistress of Henry II, daughter of a baron who held lands on the Welsh border. Henry's affair with her began after the imprisonment of Eleanor in 1173. She died soon after Henry publicly acknowledged her as his mistress, and was buried with great pomp at Godstow nunnery. Later writers described how Eleanor had found Rosamond's secret hiding place, a chamber set in a maze at Woodstock, and had poisoned her; and the chroniclers also gave her a famous epitaph belonging to an earlier Rosamond, a sixth-century Italian queen, so that her story, about which we know little for certain, soon grew into a legend.

FitzUrse, Reginald One of the murderers of Thomas Becket, often said to be the ringleader; he certainly acted as spokesman in the interview between the four knights and the archbishop. He and his accomplices fled to Scotland after the murder, but were forced to return to England. Later stories told how they died miserable deaths, after going to Palestine to do penance, but there is evidence that at least one of them lived on to a peaceful old age.

Foliot, Gilbert, bishop of London A learned and eloquent monk, related to the earl of Hereford, Foliot became bishop of London in 1163. He had opposed Becket's election as archbishop in the previous year, and on becoming bishop of London claimed that he owed no obedience to Canterbury. He and Becket became bitter enemies, as Foliot acted as the king's chief adviser on church matters during Becket's exile. He helped to crown the young king in June 1170. He died in 1187.

Frederick Barbarossa Frederick 'Barbarossa' was elected king of the Romans in 1152 and crowned at Rome in 1155. He ruled until his death in Asia Minor on the Third Crusade in 1190, and his long reign was one of the most remarkable in medieval German history. Like many medieval German emperors, he was deeply involved in Italian affairs, but conflicts with the papacy and internal revolts in Germany prevented him from fulfilling his imperial ambitions. He supported the anti-pope Victor IV against Alexander III in the schism of 1159, and in 1178 duke Henry of Saxony (Henry II's son-in-law) rebelled against him. Yet in the 1180s he was able to establish general peace in his domains, and his era remained in men's minds in later centuries as a kind of golden age. His death was a major blow to the hopes of the Crusaders, as many of his army returned home.

Glanville, Ranulph Glanville was sheriff of Lancashire in 1173 when the 'great rebellion' broke out, and it was he who, with Robert de Stuteville, commanded the northern troops who captured William the Lion at Alnwick in July 1174. By 1180 he had risen to become chief justiciar of England. He acted as John's tutor, and seems to have been as versatile as Henry himself, 'ready at short notice to lead an army, negotiate a peace, hold a council, decide a cause'. He went on crusade with Richard, and died at Acre in October 1190. A famous law treatise is said to have been written by him.

Henry VI, emperor of Germany The son of Frederick Barbarossa, Henry was fond of hunting and had a reputation as a poet; some of his poems survived. He spent much of his career fighting for the Sicilian inheritance of his wife, Constance, and his reign was also marked by continuing disturbances in Germany. Richard's ransom enabled him to mount a new expedition to Sicily, and he was crowned king in December 1194. He died on a third Sicilian journey in 1197.

Leicester, Robert, earl of An important figure in the civil wars of Stephen's reign, Robert, earl of Leicester, became Henry's first chief justiciar, jointly with Richard de Lucy, at the beginning of his reign. He acted as viceroy from 1158-63, again with de Lucy, and was the chief spokesman in the secular proceedings against Becket in 1164, though he did his best to reconcile king and archbishop. He died in 1168.

Leopold I, duke of Austria Leopold became duke of Austria in 1177, some thirty years after it had first become a duchy. He went on the Third Crusade, and rallied the German troops after the death of Frederick Barbarossa. It was as leader of the Germans that he planted his standard on the walls of Acre beside those of Richard and Philip, only to see it thrown down by the English. It was for this insult that he imprisoned Richard on his journey home.

Longchamp, William Longchamp became Richard's chancellor in Aquitaine in the late 1180s, and on Richard's accession became bishop of Ely and chancellor of England. He became chief justiciar jointly with Hugh Puiset, bishop of Durham, on Richard's departure in 1190, but managed to secure Puiset's dismissal shortly afterwards. He also became papal legate in the same year. His stern government was marred by his greed, and led to considerable popular support for a revolt by John in 1191. He was deposed in October, but remained chancellor, and was restored to some degree of favor on Richard's return in 1194. He died in 1195.

Lucy, Richard de Joint chief justiciar with Robert of Leicester from 1153-68; de Lucy continued as sole justiciar after Leicester's death in 1168, until 1179, when he resigned just before he himself died. During the quarrel with Becket, he was excommunicated by the archbishop for his support of the king. He played a very important part in the suppression of the rebellion of 1173-4, winning the battle of Fornham.

Lusignan, Hugh of The Lusignan family, who held considerable lands south-west of Poitiers, were traditional rivals of the counts of Poitou, and this rivalry continued throughout the time that the Angevins held Poitou. In 1168 they killed the governor of the county, Patrick, earl of Salisbury, in an ambush (in which the young William Marshal distinguished himself by a brave defence, and was ransomed by Eleanor). Richard fought them at intervals during his time in Aquitaine, but made friends with them when they accompanied him on the Third Crusade. John's treatment of Hugh, beginning with his marriage to Isabella of Angoulême when she was betrothed to Hugh, led to an appeal to Philip of France for aid, and hence to the loss of John's lands on the continent. Hugh was captured by John at Mirebeau in 1202, but eventually made his peace with John in 1214, when John's daughter Joan was married to one of Hugh's sons. After John's death, in 1220, he married Isabella of Angoulême, and both played a prominent part in Poitevin intrigues in Henry III's reign.

Maurienne, Humbert, count of The lands of Maurienne lay in what is now called Savoy, and included the vital passes across the Alps. Humbert had no sons, and was anxious to raise money to go on crusade, so arranged a match between his daughter and John in return for a payment of 5000 marks (just over £3000). The match fell through because Henry's attempts to provide lands for John led to the rebellion of 1173-4.

Mercadier The most famous mercenary captain of the late twelfth century; he first appears in Poitou in 1184 in Richard's service. He distinguished himself in the brief campaign in Berry in 1194, and was active in northern France in 1197-9. He was with Richard at Châlus, and after Richard's injury took the castle.

Roches, Peter des, bishop of Winchester Peter des Roches was one of Richard's chamberlains, and came originally from Poitou. He acted for John in Poitou and in negotiations with Philip of France. He was elected bishop of Winchester in 1205, and was a staunch supporter of the king throughout the interdict. He was unpopular with the barons, both as an administrator and as a foreigner, and was responsible for excommunicating the leaders of the barons in the summer of 1215. He played an important military part in the civil war of 1216-17, helping William Marshal to win the crucial victory at Lincoln in May 1217. He later went on the crusade led by Frederick II in 1228-31, and on his return became the chief power in the land until his downfall in 1234. He died in 1238.

Roches, William des The most powerful baron in Anjou at the beginning of John's reign, he at first opposed John, but later helped him to capture Arthur at Mirebeau, on condition that he should have a say in Arthur's fate. When Arthur was taken, John refused to let des Roches have any control over him, and des Roches went over to the French side. In 1214 he checked John's victorious progress into Anjou by holding out at Roches-au-Moine.

Safadin Al-adil, or Safadin, was the brother of the great Saracen general Saladin, Richard's opponent in Palestine. In 1191, in an effort to reach a peace settlement, Richard suggested that Safadin should marry Joanna, his sister. Saladin treated the proposal as a joke, but Richard was serious and was deterred only when Joanna refused to marry a Moslem, and Safadin declined to become a Christian. He later became Sultan of Egypt and, just after his death, his forces captured Louis IX on the Fifth Crusade.

Saladin Saladin, Richard's great opponent in Palestine, was remarkable both as a general and politician. He served the caliph Nur-ed-din until the latter's death in 1174, but then changed his allegiance to the orthodox caliph at Baghdad, and was proclaimed sultan of Egypt. From 1174-86, he conquered Syria, encircling the Christian kingdom of Jerusalem with his own lands, and in 1187, after his overwhelming victory at the Horns of Hattin, he took Jerusalem. Within months of Richard's departure, he died at Damascus, but Richard's inability to follow up his military successes with a new political settlement meant that Saladin's successors were able to hold off the Christians and retain Jerusalem.

Salisbury, William 'Longespée', earl of William 'Longsword', earl of

Salisbury, was the illegitimate son of Henry II by an unknown mother. He married the heiress to the earldom of Salisbury in 1198, and was a close associate of John throughout his reign, acting as military commander and diplomat as well as administrator. In 1213 he commanded the naval force which overwhelmed the French invasion fleet at Damme, and in the civil war was one of John's chief supporters until the arrival of Louis of France in 1216. He died in 1226.

Theobald Theobald, who became abbot of the important Norman monastery of Bec in 1137, was elected archbishop of Canterbury in 1138. He had difficulties with Stephen's brother, Henry of Blois, who had hoped to become archbishop himself, but nonetheless managed to defend the rights of Canterbury and to make it an important center of learning where men such as Robert of Pont l'Evêque (later archbishop of York) and Thomas Becket himself were trained. In 1148 he attended a church council at Rheims despite Stephen's ban, and was sent into exile for much of that year. He favored the Angevin cause, and in 1152 refused to crown Stephen's son Eustace, an action that helped to ensure Henry's succession. In 1154, he crowned Henry and Eleanor at Westminster, and became one of Henry's chief advisers in the years immediately after his accession. He died in April 1161.

Ventadour, Bernard of One of the leading poets of the troubadour movement in southern France. One of his poems was addressed to Eleanor of Aquitaine, and later biographers elaborated on this, making him Eleanor's lover. His poems are delicate and refined, seeing the relationship between lover and beloved as a feudal one, distant and frustrating, but he shows how 'joy d'amour,' the lover's ecstasy, can be increased by this very frustration and despair.

Walter, Hubert Brought up in Ranulf Glanville's household (see above), Walter was employed from the first in the royal service. He went on crusade with Richard, and assumed archbishop Baldwin's role after the latter's death. On his return he was elected archbishop of Canterbury in 1193, and became justiciar in the same year. He was responsible for the government of England in Richard's absence, and suppressed John's attempt at revolt early in 1194. He also played a leading part in raising Richard's ransom. He resigned as justiciar on the pope's instructions in 1198, but played an important part in keeping the peace in England after Richard's death. He crowned John in May 1199, and became chancellor the day after the coronation, a post which he retained except for a brief interval until his death in 1205.

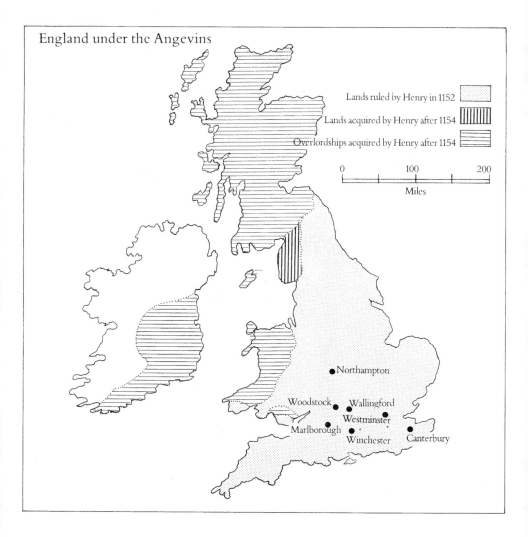

England under the Angevins

Lands ruled by Henry in 1152
Lands acquired by Henry after 1154
Overlordships acquired by Henry after 1154

0   100   200
Miles

● Northampton

Woodstock ● ● Wallingford
● Westminster
Marlborough ●
Winchester ● ● Canterbury

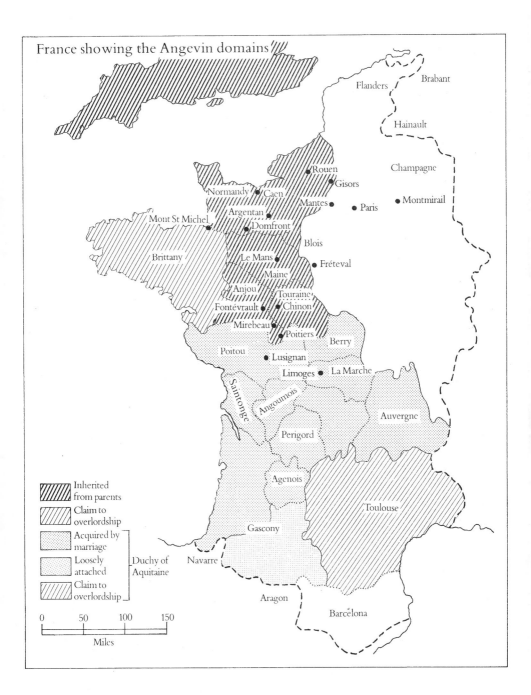

France showing the Angevin domains

Legend:
- Inherited from parents
- Claim to overlordship
- Acquired by marriage
- Loosely attached
- Claim to overlordship

Duchy of Aquitaine

Miles
0 50 100 150

Flanders, Brabant, Hainault, Champagne

Rouen, Gisors, Montmirail, Normandy, Caen, Mantes, Paris, Argentan, Domfront, Mont St Michel, Blois, Brittany, Le Mans, Fréteval, Maine, Anjou, Touraine, Fontévrault, Chinon, Mirebeau, Poitiers, Berry, Poitou, Lusignan, Saintonge, Limoges, La Marche, Angoumois, Auvergne, Perigord, Agenois, Toulouse, Gascony, Navarre, Aragon, Barcelona

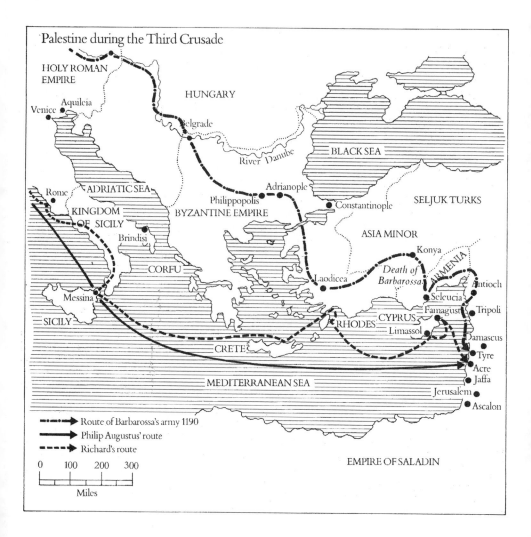

Palestine during the Third Crusade

HOLY ROMAN
EMPIRE

HUNGARY

Venice
Aquileia
Belgrade

River Danube

BLACK SEA

Rome
ADRIATIC SEA

KINGDOM
OF SICILY

Brindisi

CORFU

Messina

SICILY

CRETE

MEDITERRANEAN SEA

Philippopolis

BYZANTINE EMPIRE

Adrianople

Constantinople

SELJUK TURKS

ASIA MINOR

Konya

Laodicea

Death of
Barbarossa

ARMENIA

Seleucia

Antioch

Famagusta

Tripoli

RHODES

CYPRUS

Limassol

Damascus

Tyre

Acre

Jaffa

Jerusalem

Ascalon

▪▪▪▪➤ Route of Barbarossa's army 1190
──➤ Philip Augustus' route
▬ ▬ ➤ Richard's route

0   100   200   300

Miles

EMPIRE OF SALADIN

178

Richard's journey home through
the Adriatic, Austria and Germany

Boundary of Holy Roman Empire ▪ ▪ ▪ ▪
Richard's journey before
his arrest by Leopold ➤
Castles where Richard ✦
was imprisoned

0   50   100   150   200
Miles

SAXONY

FLANDERS
BRABANT   Cologne
THURINGIA
Mainz
Wurzburg   R. Main   Prague   POLAND
FRANCONIA Worms   BOHEMIA
Trifels Speyer Ochsenfurt   MORAVIA
LORRAINE   AUSTRIA
Hagenau   Regensburg   Dürrenstein ✦
FRANCE   SWABIA   R. Danube   Vienna
R. Rhine   STYRIA
BAVARIA   HUNGARY

KINGDOM OF
BURGUNDY
(OR ARLES)
Venice Aquileia
Verona   Gorz

KINGDOM OF ITALY

PROVENCE
Arles
ADRIATIC SEA

1. The Norman and Angevin Kings

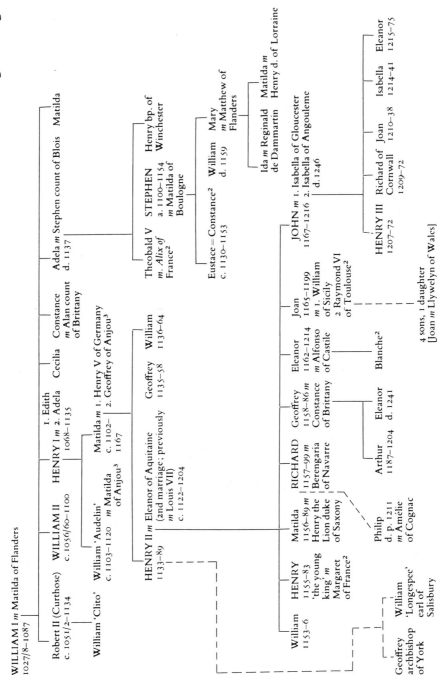

2. The Kings of France

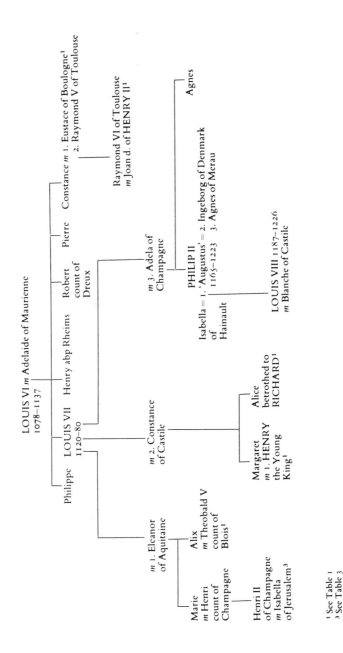

3. The House of Anjou and the Kings of Jerusalem

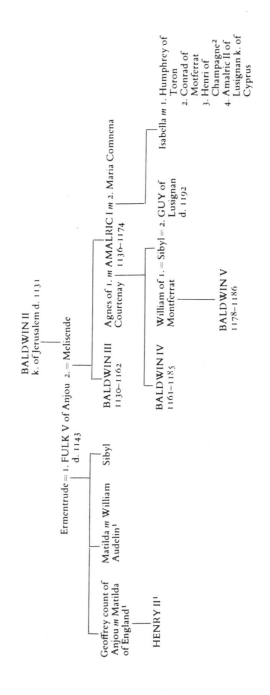

[1] See Table 1
[2] See Table 2

Further Reading

Biographies

WARREN, W.L. *Henry II* (London 1973, reissued 1977), English Monarch series.

BARBER, RICHARD Henry Plantagenent (London 1964, reissued 1973).

APPLEBY, JOHN Henry II: The Vanquished King (London 1963).

KELLY, AMY *Eleanor of Aquitaine and the Four Kings* (Cambridge, Mass. 1950). Old-fashioned, romantic but nonetheless scholarly biography; a brief more recent book is that by Régine Pernoud (*Eleanor of Aquitaine*, London 1976). The best summary of Eleanor's character is Edmond-René Labande's article (in French) 'Pour une image véridique d' Aliénor d' Aquitaine: *Bulletin de la Société des Antiquaires de l'Ouest* 4. II (1952) 173-233.

NORGATE, KATE *Richard Coeur de Lion* (London 1924). Still the best biography of Richard available.

GILLINGHAM, JOHN *The Life and Times of Richard I* (London 1973): *Richard I* (London 1978).

HENDERSON, PHILIP *Richard Coeur de Lion* (London 1958).

WARREN, W.L. *King John* (London 1961, reissued 1966). Less substantial than his *Henry II*, but in fact equally good as a biography.

NORGATE, KATE *John Lackland* (London (1962).

HOLT, J.C. *King John* (London 1963).

ASHLEY, MAURICE *The Life and Times of King John* (London 1972).

PAINTER, SIDNEY *The Reign of King John* (Baltimore 1952).

PAINTER, SIDNEY *William Marshal* (London 1933).

Novels and plays

DUGGAN, ALFLRED *The Devil's Brood; God and My Right.*

GRAHAM, WINSTON *Becket.*

ANOUILH, Jean *Becket.*

GOLDMAN, JAMES *The Lion in Winter.*

ELIOT, T.S. *Murder in the Cathedral.*

HEWLETT, MAURICE *Richard Yea and Nay.*

Index

Persons are indexed under forenames, as it is often difficult to disinguish between true surnames and changing titles.